EYES OPENED
INTO THE
Supernatural
WORLD!

Permetrice Milroe Jackson

EYES OPENED Into The Supernatural World!

Scriptures are from the King James Version and the New King James Version of the Bible. The Hebrew and Greek definitions are from the James E. Strong Exhaustive Concordance. The English definitions were taken from the Merriam-Webster Dictionary.

The testimonies included in this book are all true. The author has shared them to teach and clarify about the reality of the supernatural world. This book will also encourage and enlighten you about God's miracle-working power to heal us, to save us from danger, explain about God's ability to reveal his will to us, and his decision to bless people with EYES OPENED into the realm of the Spirit. It is the author's desire that you will be richly blessed by EYES OPENED Into The Supernatural World!

Published by:
Passion Peach Publishing
1333 Cedar Grove Road, #203
Conley, Georgia 30288

Library of Congress Control Number: 2021907036

Author Photo Credit: Harry's Digital, Inc. Atlanta, GA

Printed in the United States of America

ISBN 978-1-886815-14-8
eBook ISBN 978-1-886815-15-5

Other Books by Permetrice Milroe Jackson

Rejoice After Rejection!

Available at BarnesandNoble.com, Walmart.com, Booksamillion.com, Amazon.com, Apple Books and other online sites. (Paperback and eBook)

Duplicity: Double Life Drama
A Novel

280 Pages of Suspense, Romance and Drama
Available at BarnesandNoble.com, Walmart.com, Booksamillion.com, Amazon.com and other online sites. (Paperback and eBook)

Effective Prayers in Jesus' Name

Available at BarnesandNoble.com, Walmart.com, Amazon.com, Booksamillion.com, Apple Books and other online sites. (Paperback and eBook)

Dedication

I dedicate this book to my wonderful Mother, Gwendolyn Jolly Milroe who is the epitome of grace, sophistication, and class. She is such an awesome parent who loved and nurtured me in a phenomenal way! I am thankful that I had a wonderful example which allowed me to become a great mother. She is a retired teacher who not only positively influenced my life, but also countless students in Chicago Public Schools.

I also dedicate this to my children: Roger L. Jackson, Jr., Jaleese Jackson, and Kirsten Jackson. Each of you have gifts and talents that I believe the world will celebrate one day. Be encouraged and know that I love you!

Finally, I dedicate this book to Taylor, my "Precious" granddaughter from my son. After she read the first two chapters of the manuscript, she said, "You described the angels so clearly that I could really see them. I love the book!" I really feel that her heartfelt, fourteen-year-old compliment and her request for me to hurry and finish writing it so she could read the entire book, truly confirmed this anointed, intriguing, and inspirational release!

Acknowledgements

I thank my beta readers, Caroline Allen, Kirsten Jackson, and Jean McCoy, for their diligent proofreading, suggestions and faithful support of **EYES OPENED Into The Supernatural World!**
I appreciate my wonderful editor and friend, Author Merisa Parson Davis! Thank you for your time and attention to detail to help me finalize this anointed and inspirational book.
To my family, friends, and hosts of readers, I thank you for your love, prayers, and support!

I want to encourage every person who has suffered the devastation of relationship rejection. Although your situation may have been negative, I want you to know that "trouble does not last always" and you will come out better than before the disappointment. Reach for the stars and realize that your great destiny is not contingent on those who left you, or for whom you chose to leave. God wants the best for you and your best days are ahead of you!

I Praise God the Father, Jesus the Son of God, and the Spirit of God for the calling on my life to Preach the Gospel, to write novels to entertain you, and inspirational books to encourage you!

EYES OPENED Into The Supernatural World!

Table of Contents

Dedication

Acknowledgements

Introduction

Permetrice Milroe Jackson

Table of Contents

Introduction

Since you are reading this book, I know you have natural sight. Some of you may require glasses or contact lenses to assist you. Either way, the words on these pages and other natural things within your view are clearly visible. I also realize that you apparently have an interest in knowing about the supernatural world. You are about to embark on a literary and testimonial journey that I believe will enlighten and encourage you!

I want this book to inspire you and to solidify your faith in the existence of other spiritual forces that God uses to help you! I believe you will enjoy the intriguing accounts and the vivid descriptions of the supernatural beings that I have literally observed from the "unseen" world. As you read my testimony and the miraculous experiences on these insightful pages, I pray that you will be richly blessed! I give God all the Praise and Glory for his power and authority to intervene in and to guide our lives! Our God truly is an Awesome God!

A Little About My Journey

I was blessed with loving parents, Clarence and Gwendolyn Jolly Milroe. My father was from Baton Rouge, LA. He migrated to Chicago, Illinois for better job opportunities. My mother was born in Hernando, MS and raised in Coldwater, MS and Memphis, TN. Her parents wanted her to get a better education, so she attended high school in the Windy City. They met, married, and purchased an empty lot and had a lovely three-bedroom, brick home with a finished basement built in a nice middle-class neighborhood. I have two older siblings and a younger sister. My older sister was four when they moved in the house. My brother was born a year later. I came on the scene three years after him, and my younger sister is eight years younger than me.

Unfortunately, I was born premature with a very low birth weight. The pediatric doctor told my parents that I had little chance of surviving. My parents prayed for me and thank God, I not only survived, I thrived! My parents took me to church where I was christened, baptized, and dedicated to the Lord at an early age.

My father told me that I was so tiny that he could hold me in the palm of one hand. He often told me when the doctor stated that I had little chance of surviving, my "Daddy" would tear up when he thought back to that time and say, "…But, I prayed for you." My mother also prayed, and I believe God honored their prayers, for the Lord had a purpose in mind for my life. I know angels, God's ministering Spirits from Heaven, watched over me as I was growing up.

Not only was there a negative prognosis when I was born, but I had some near-death experiences where the devil tried to kill me. He had a glimpse into my destiny and purpose, but God has been faithful to keep me safe to fulfill his will for my life!

* * *

I vividly remember being at Rainbow Beach which is part of Lake Michigan because it was a common pastime for my family. The lake is so beautiful and peaceful! During one of those visits, while spending time with my family when I was five years old, I almost drowned in Lake Michigan!

There were family members around my brother and me as we played in the shallow water. Apparently, we went out too far, not knowing the power of the currents. I felt myself being pulled down under the waves as I inhaled and swallowed water. It was a terrible experience and I was afraid because I could not see my family anymore, as I swallowed more water. I desperately tried to grab someone as I was sinking further into the depths of the lake. I didn't really understand what was happening to me because I was so young.

I thank God that my Mother noticed that I was missing, miraculously found me, and pulled me to safety! Someone pumped my stomach and I survived! I vividly remember this terrifying incident.

A few years later, the devil tried to drown me again. While I was on a vacation as an eight-year-old, I was in the shallow, four-feet deep end of a large swimming pool, splashing water and playing with my cousins in Memphis, Tennessee.

I had some fear as I recalled what happened in Lake Michigan. While enjoying the cool water and the fun and games, I relaxed and soon followed my cousins, who were good swimmers, further toward the middle of the pool not realizing that the water was getting higher. Before I knew it, the floor of the pool was no longer under my feet and I started going under once again! Unfortunately, I did not know how to swim, and I was frightened! I had flashbacks of when I almost drowned the first time!

My arms flailed in the water as I attempted to grab something, but nothing was near as I once again swallowed too much water, sinking further down. One young cousin finally noticed my dilemma and tried to rescue me. In a panic, I pressed down on his shoulders pushing him under water as I tried to get above the surface!

Miraculously, he was able to pull me out of the pool and his mother performed mouth to mouth resuscitation and pumped by stomach as I gurgled and coughed up the excess water. I thank the Lord Jesus that I was rescued again!

While enjoying EYES OPENED Into The Supernatural World, you will read about other near-death experiences that I have had and dangerous situations that I have encountered. I thank God that you will also read about the Angelic interventions from the unseen realm that supernaturally protected or rescued me! The devil had a plot, but God had a plan, and saved my life every time! This reminds me of a Scripture in Jeremiah 29:11 which says, "For I know the thoughts that I think toward you, says the LORD, thoughts of peace, and not of evil, to give you an expected end." This "expected end" means God has a planned, strategic, deliberate journey and great ultimate destiny for his people!

One thing I know for sure is that I serve an Awesome God who has called me for a great and intentional purpose! I gave my life to Jesus Christ at sixteen years old and I will spend the rest of my life serving him. I Praise God for using me as a Preacher, Evangelist, Poet, Educator, Actress, and an Author to bless others. It is an honor and a pleasure to offer my life, gifts, and talents to serve The All Mighty Living God!

Permetrice Milroe Jackson

Chapter 1

Close Encounters

As we navigate through this journey of life, we meet many people from a host of different backgrounds. We meet some people who merely become acquaintances and others who we may build platonic friendships. Perhaps we will choose a few individuals that we will develop special, long-term close friendships or even deeper relationships with others. God created us as social beings and these various relationships are natural and beneficial for our mental and emotional well-being.

Have you ever wondered if other beings are on earth with us? Do you think about the idea that there are angels and demons that you cannot see with your natural eyes? It is an intriguing question and the Bible gives us details about these entities.

The unseen spiritual realm or world is as real as the natural world! There is a plethora of Scriptures in the Word of God, the Bible, to substantiate the reality of and the belief in the unseen, supernatural world. We read in 2 Corinthians 4:18, "While we look not at the things which are seen, but at the things which are not seen: for the things which are seen are temporary; but the things which are not seen are eternal." In other words, there is a permanent and unending presence and the reality of a supernatural existence of spiritual beings and eternal places: Hell and Heaven.

This book will focus on the miraculous preeminence of God and on the things that are invisible to your natural eyes unless God allows you to see into the supernatural world. Although the Bible teaches and confirms the existence of angelic beings, I can testify that I have had supernatural experiences that I hope will encourage you to believe what the Bible says!

EYES OPENED Into The Supernatural World! includes extraordinary miracles that I have experienced or witnessed. Some were miracles of healing and others were phenomenal interventions from accidents or attacks. I explicitly explain and share prophetic dreams that revealed sensitive information about people who lived near me or in distant areas of the country. I will also clearly describe spectacular, detailed revelations of a majestic, Heavenly mansion as well as the heated and horrible demonic terrors that I saw reference to Hell!

You may have heard about or read about angels and demons. Personally, I can attest to the existence of angels and demons although I must admit that I prefer seeing and writing about angelic beings who are on our side and mean us well. I will share a powerful personal account of seeing these majestic beings! I truly believe you will be richly encouraged after reading the vivid descriptions of these impressive Heavenly hosts and their positive influence on us. I will also share information on evil spirits and demons and their negative impact on people.

In this book, I have included some powerful testimonies of modern-day miracles because some of you stand in need of a miracle. What better way to believe for God to intervene, but to read about what God has done for somebody else in the Bible as well as in modern times? These are real life miracles that nobody can explain or rationalize away. I was blessed to observe the accounts first-hand. It is an honor to share the vivid details with you.

There are amazing miracles in the Bible that will encourage you. The scriptures about miracles when Jesus walked the earth will teach you or perhaps remind you of God's Divine deliverance power! The supernatural experiences that I have witnessed, testify of the Lord's ability to take Bible-based divine blessings off the pages of the Word of God into modern-day demonstrations of God's power. God's Word says in Revelations 12:11, "And they overcame him (the devil), by the blood of the lamb and by the word of their testimony." I have shared these miracles and powerful revelations because when you need the

Lord to move on your behalf, you will be able to pray to God about your need, but also say, "God, if you did it for Permetrice Milroe Jackson, you can do it for me!"

Some of my encounters with supernatural beings and miraculous experiences are from years ago and some are recent events. The important thing to remember is that they are all true. God has now released me to reveal these special experiences by sharing them with you. I want this book to help solidify your faith in the Word of God and how he uses his ministers and angels on earth to bless you! His demonstrated power is still available on earth for those who believe in and trust our Awesome and Mighty Heavenly Father!

For those who may still have some doubts after reading these testimonies of the supernatural world, it is okay because whether you believe or not, they are all real and true. Be encouraged and know that God loves you and he is allowing me to share these events. It is another example of his grace and desire to encourage and inform you.

To everyone reading these real testimonies, it is my prayer that you will gain knowledge, be inspired and truly enjoy this book, EYES OPENED Into The Supernatural World! Please buckle up for an amazing ride into the marvelous, miraculous, and supernatural realm of the Spirit!

Chapter 2

Angels All Around Us

There are angels all around us, watching over us. There are also angels assigned to each of us by God Almighty. It is up to you to believe in their existence and welcome their help and protection from danger. An Associated Press poll in 2011 reflected that 77% of adults and 95% of Christians believe that, "Angels exist and influence people's lives." Do you believe?

God is in control of our lives and he has the authority and power to use the abilities of his angels to deliver messages to us, and to protect or deliver us from danger. Angels can be assigned other tasks that the Lord deems necessary to bless our lives.

Since angels are purposefully powerful and instrumental on earth, you may wonder whether we should praise angels. No. We are not to worship or praise angels, human beings, or any other created entity. While it is appropriate to appreciate, honor, and respect people, God the Father and Jesus Christ deserve all praise, worship, and glory!

EYES OPENED Into The Supernatural World!

The Purpose of Angels

Have you ever wondered why God created angels and what purpose they serve? God created angels for many purposes. We will explain some of them for your edification and understanding of these celestial beings.

Angels are Heavenly beings created by God to be a blessing to us and to fulfill his purpose on earth. It is a blessing to have God send an angel in response to our prayers or in our time of need. Psalm 34:7-9 says, "The angel of the Lord encamps around those who fear (or give reverence to) him, and he delivers them. Taste and see that the Lord is good; blessed is the one who trusts him. Fear the Lord, you his holy people, for those who fear him lack nothing." This is a powerful Scripture! Those who "fear" or reference God will have their needs met. Philippians 4:19 says, "…But my God shall supply all your need according to his riches in glory by Christ Jesus." In addition to all of this, we know one name for God is Jehovah-Jireh which means, "The Lord will provide!" Know that whatever you require, God can supply the need even if it involves the assistance of angels!

God created angels as benevolent celestial beings who act as intermediaries between God and his people. They serve as protection for us, many times intervening to keep you from danger or physical harm. Angels can also guide human beings out of dangerous situations so that you are not a victim of a random act of violence or other attack.

God assigns angels to strengthen us. Jesus was physically sick in the Garden of Gethsemane because the devil didn't want him to make it to the Cross! The Plan of Salvation was already established in Heaven. Jesus was to be beaten with 39 stripes, shed his blood, and willingly suffer and die an excruciating death on the Cross for our sins! The devil knew the plan and he attacked Jesus in the Garden of Gethsemane on the Mount of Olives. God used an angel to minister strength to our Lord and Savior according to the Scripture, Luke 22:43-44. "And there appeared an angel unto him from Heaven, strengthening him. And being in an agony he prayed more earnestly: and his sweat was as great drops of blood falling down to the ground." God did not leave Jesus without help and he will help us in our time of need. It is comforting to know that we are not alone. Besides having angelic hosts to strengthen and help protect us, Jesus promised in Matthew 28:20 that "… I am with you always even until the end of the world." Thank God!

Angels carry out tasks on behalf of God. Have you ever been in a painful situation and suddenly you felt a strong sense of comfort come over you? That feeling was either the Spirit of God, the Holy Ghost or perhaps an angel sent to comfort you in your time of need.

EYES OPENED Into The Supernatural World!

Have you ever wondered what angels do to enhance your everyday life? Sometimes, God sends angels to comfort you. In Hebrews 1:14, we find this scripture, "Are not all angels ministering spirits sent to serve those who will inherit salvation?" When you are sad or hurting in your spirit, your phone may not ring, but God may send angels to help you feel better. Angelic hosts may be in church services praising the Lord and providing comfort to people in a blessed congregation. Sometimes these angels will appear or reveal themselves to some people who are worshiping, but other people may not have a clue that they are visiting. Angels may even visit a congregation to provide strategic and supernatural security, effectively blocking a demonic attack.

Although rare, angels can take on the form of flesh like human beings for a purpose, so be careful how you treat people. Hebrews 13:2 says, "Do not forget to entertain (acknowledge) strangers, for by so doing, some people have entertained angels without knowing it."

Sometimes, angels are sent to you by God to intervene on your behalf when the enemy, the devil meant for a catastrophe to harm, destroy, or even kill you or one of your beloved family members.

I heard a story about a four-year-old toddler who fell out of a fifth-floor apartment window to certain death. The mother screamed, panicked, and quickly got outside in a frantic race to help her child.

She didn't see him on the ground but when he called her, she looked up at him sitting on a limb of a tree that was not right next to the building. The fire department was called and when the fireman rescued the boy, he also noticed that the tree was not in direct proximity to the window. He noted that the child was not injured and that he appeared very calm. As the grateful mother approached her son, he said, "The big stranger's hand caught me and put me in the tree."

This vivid description was an innocent toddler's view and account of an angelic being because no human was tall enough or fast enough to grab him as he plummeted towards the ground. Although nobody witnessed what happened, this was a miraculous rescue by an angel who God used to save the child's life! Thank God for his miraculous intervention!

Angels realize the majesty of God and they willingly praise and worship him. In Revelations 4:8, we find that angels stand at the Holy Seat and praise and worship God day and night saying, "…Holy, holy, holy is the Lord God Almighty, who was, and is, and is to come."

EYES OPENED Into The Supernatural World!

An Angel Intervened

I was on vacation walking from a store in my childhood neighborhood, in the Windy City of Chicago, Illinois. Although I am normally very responsible and alert; however, that day I was so happy to be back home that apparently, at that moment, I was distracted. I did not see what was coming ...

I was one city block from my Mother's house when I stepped off the curb onto a side street. I made approximately four steps when suddenly, I was snatched backward by my shoulders and upper arms with enough force that I was literally lifted from the street back onto the curb and sidewalk!

As soon as my feet hit the curb and sidewalk again, an automobile sped past me through the spot that I had just been snatched from! The driver was speeding and moving along the edge of the curb instead of the middle of the one-way side street! Instantly, I knew I would have been killed if the car had hit me because the violent impact would have been too catastrophic to survive.

I was very shaken up in those few seconds and grateful that the person behind me had the concern, quick action, and the strength to pull me out of harm's way. Of course, I wanted to thank the kind stranger for pulling me away from the speeding car.

I immediately turned around while saying, "Thank you for..." Abruptly, I stopped talking because there was absolutely nobody behind me on the sidewalk or on the lawn! I was stunned! I quickly raised my hands in praise to God; and verbally thanked him because he had sent an angel to deliver me from being a victim of a reckless driver! I didn't see the car, but God saw it! God knew the danger and delivered me from it with his divine protection!

This was a miraculous intervention! Think about it. I literally felt my body lifted from the lower surface of the street to the curb and sidewalk, yet no human being was behind or around me! This was a modern-day miracle! Hallelujah to the Most, High God!

In the next chapter, I will share another amazing testimony where angels intervened and saved my college classmate and me from two immoral men who threatened to abduct and molest us!

He Opened My Eyes
(And... Literally, I Saw Angels!)

I was in the audience of a church listening to a lady give a speech in the small city of Forest Park, which is south of the city of Atlanta, Georgia. The woman was speaking for about ten minutes when I noticed a very bright orange-yellowish light radiating at the top and the sides of her head! Within seconds, the light outlined her entire body! The glow was about eight inches wide. As she made periodic movements, the glow also moved. The glow or illumination was in-sync with her. I realized that it was her spiritual aura, which is normally invisible, but God allowed me to see it!

As I processed the sight of her aura, suddenly, a huge angel stood behind her! The angel was facing the audience. I was shocked because I had never seen an angel with my own eyes! I blinked because I truly thought I was "seeing things!" When I opened my eyes, the angel was still standing there behind her. I then shook my head to attempt to clear my vision, closing my eyes again in the process. I opened my eyes to see the angel turn its head toward its right and my left to reveal a perfect human-looking profile.

Suddenly, a second angel appeared, walked down the center isle toward the right of the woman and stood near the piano on the platform. It then turned to look toward the stained-glass window. The angels appeared and were visible to me in the same way that I could see the people. I looked at my husband to determine by his expression if he was noticing the glorious Heavenly beings that I clearly saw in the church building. He sat oblivious to what was going on and later stated that he did not see the angels.

I decided that I was not going to say a word to anyone until after church was over because I did not want to disturb the service.

Just like the United States, our congregation was racially diverse. An elderly Caucasian lady stood up minutes before the service was over and asked the leader, "Pastor, may I say something?" He yielded the floor and gave her permission to talk. While standing at her seat she stated, "I didn't want to disturb the service, but as my sister was speaking, I saw a glow around her. Then a beautiful angel appeared behind her. Another angel walked on the platform, stood there and then turned to look at the window."

As soon as the elderly lady gave her testimony about seeing the angels, another woman who was middle-aged and Native American stood to confirm that she also saw them.

After the two women testified, I decided to stand and boldly proclaim that I was blessed to see the Heavenly visitors as well. I stood and said, "I was not going to say anything until after the service, but I saw the angels too." I explained that I saw the bright glow or aura around the woman while she talked. I described the massive angel that stood behind her the entire time that she delivered her speech. Of course, I mentioned the second angel that I also saw.

EYES OPENED Into The Supernatural World!

Seeing those magnificent angels was an amazing experience and I thank the Lord that he chose me, and two others to confirm their presence. I am also grateful that God has finally directed me to share the experience with you.

The Bible says in 2 Corinthians 13:1, "...Through the mouth of two or three witnesses, let every word be established." The existence of and the sighting of the angels by the three of us confirmed God's word that they exist and that they were in the church service that day. God allowed our, "EYES OPENED" and revealed this wonderful truth by allowing us to have the experience of seeing angelic hosts supernaturally! The following is a vivid and thorough description of the angels!

Angels Are Amazing

The Heavenly Angels that I saw that day stood about nine to ten feet tall. Their massive width cannot be overstated. They looked like bulked quadruple-sized, linebacker football players, without jerseys or shoulder pads. To estimate their width, I would guess they were approximately five to six feet wide! Although they did not have skin color, they had facial features just like human beings. Their eyes had brilliance without a noted color.

The angel who turned to look out the stained-glass window revealed a perfect facial profile like a human being, but appeared both, transparent and translucent. I noticed perfect eyes, nose, mouth, cheeks, and forehead. To put the description of angels into terms that are easier to understand, I would say that their bodies looked similar to the Hollywood depiction of Casper the Friendly Ghost. In other words, they had mass and depth without skin, fat, or material clothes. The angels' garments were big, flowing, white, yet transparent robes. The angels were clear, massive, impressive, and Heavenly – all at the same time. Seeing the angels was truly an amazing and life changing experience!

Of course, I had read about angels in the Bible and I had heard various preachers deliver sermons about them. I was taught about their amazing existence and their ability to conduct spiritual warfare on our behalf; therefore, I believed by faith that angels existed. After that special Sunday, I not only have the scriptural references about angels, but I have seen them with my own eyes! God opened my natural eyes and allowed me to see into the supernatural world or realm!

To be clear, these angels were as visible to me as the people who were in the church with me. Everyone was sitting down except the woman who was speaking. Of course, I saw the people, but I also was looking at the angels who were as vivid as the stained-glass windows and the pews. Most of the people did not see the angels. I was one of the blessed women that God allowed to witness the angelic hosts. To this day, I feel so honored to have seen them and I am happy to share their sighting with you. Trust me; you would want these Heavenly Angels on your side – warring or fighting for you, protecting you, ministering to your needs and in any other way, working on your behalf!

Chapter 3

A Botched Abduction!

By the end of my freshmen year of college I had formed a great friendship with a girl named Sherryl who was from Albany, Georgia. She was a kind-hearted Southern Belle with a heart of gold. Sherryl and I decided to share a dormitory room the next school year. We wanted a suite instead of a regular room because the suites had a private, full bathroom inside, instead of us having to use a communal restroom down the hall. The private college we attended, Clark College, later named Clark Atlanta University when it merged with Atlanta University, did not have many suites. We decided that we would get in line early by sitting on the steps of the administration building overnight and wait for the office to open the next day. Both of us were young and naïve and did not realize that this would not be a safe thing to do. We did not tell other students about our plan because we did not want anyone to be ahead of us in the line.

Sherryl and I walked to the building and sat down at the top of the steps, leaning our backs against the doors, determined to stay awake all night long. We talked to each other to pass the time away. She and I were happy to be the only ones there, which would guarantee we would be the first in the line the next morning.

At about 2:30a.m., we noticed two men in a long, Lincoln Continental slowly driving by. The passenger glanced at us and said something to the driver who abruptly paused the car and backed up to the front of the administration building. They stared at us as the driver stopped the vehicle in the middle of the deserted street. Then the passenger asked us, "What are you ladies doing out here at this time of night?"

Being from the big, Windy City of Chicago, I knew that we did not need to talk to these strangers. I motioned to my roommate to keep quiet, but I was too late because she did not notice my gesture.

In her sweet Southern accent, Sherryl replied, "We're waiting to sign up for a dormitory suite." Of course, these grown men knew that the office would not open until the morning, so her honest, but naïve answer meant that we intended to be out there all night. Hearing that, the driver immediately pulled over to the curb and parked the car!

The passenger then threateningly asked us, "Aren't you afraid of being molested?"

Permetrice Milroe Jackson

What? Gulp! My future roommate and I looked at each other. There was fear in Sherryl's eyes! We both knew this had now turned into a very dangerous situation!

With that explosive question, the men simultaneously, exited their vehicle and started removing large poster signs from the car's back seat and the floor! Holding some of the signs, the passenger casually opened the trunk and placed some of the posters inside. He glanced back up at us and then proceeded to clear the rest of the posters from the car, making room in the back seat for their intended victims – the two of us!

Once the men cleared the back seat, they left the passenger back door wide open for us! In unison, the men started strolling up the broad walkway toward us! Fear gripped our hearts because nobody knew we were outside on the administration building's porch, waiting for the office to open! What could we do? We were two petite, young women up against two big, tall, robust, lustful men who were determined to sexually assault us! His question of, "Aren't you afraid of being molested?" was prophetic in his mind because they intended to harm us in an unthinkable way!

Some of you may be wondering why we did not immediately call the police. Neither one of us had a cell phone, so that option was not possible.

EYES OPENED Into The Supernatural World!

From his sadistic question implying rape, to them walking along the wide sidewalk and up four steps, took just about 30 seconds, but we were filled with anxiety! I decided that I was not going to surrender to the men! Although I had to think quickly, what could I say to answer his question? Of course, I was afraid, but I was not going to let the would-be rapists know it! Sherryl and I looked at each other again. Before that moment, it never occurred to us that being first in line at all cost was a great, but naïve and foolish idea; however, the dangerous reality of the situation was now apparent. Fear tried to grip my mind as I processed how to answer his question, "Aren't you afraid of being molested?"

At that crucial moment, what choice did I have, but to lean on the Everlasting Arms of God, his Son Jesus Christ, and his Spirit the Holy Ghost! I could not be silent or overtaken by fear! Suddenly, out of the depth of my gut or soul, a strong response came up and out of my mouth with conviction, power, and authority! I boldly answered him, "NO, BECAUSE GOD IS WITH US!" It was such a strong proclamation that it almost sounded foreign to me! I did not flinch or stutter. I meant every word that came out of my mouth! In other words, I was telling those men and the demon of lust in them, *'You may be bigger and stronger than we are, and full of the devil, but My God will protect us!'*

Permetrice Milroe Jackson

As soon as I made that powerful declaration, the two would-be rapists stopped mid-step, dead-in-their-tracks! Suddenly, they both looked way above our heads with horrified expressions! Their eyes rotated from left to right, and back again with confused and fearful countenances! They were no longer looking directly in our faces as we sat on the landing with our backs to the building's doors!

Ironically, these two evil men looked terrified! The man who had asked the question, "Aren't you afraid of being molested?" started stuttering saying, "That's, that's, that's good, good...!" Their horrified eyes were focused on the Warrior Angels! They started walking backwards down those same steps that they had climbed with the intention to forcibly remove us from the building and place us in the back seat of their car! They walked down the steps backwards until they cleared the stairs and part of the broad walkway! They were still staring at the Warrior Angels that were behind and around us! After they walked backwards on the walkway for about six feet, they quickly turned around and literally ran to their car, got in and sped away from the school! They never touched us! Their intended abduction, threatened molestation, and rape were all stopped by Warrior Angels! Praise our God!

I believe the powerful words that I spoke were anointed by God and the fact that I stood on my faith in God's ability to deliver us, evoked the Warrior

Angels to immediately, show up in a real and profound way! Obviously, the two men saw them, were afraid, and they realized that we were off limits to their filthy hands and immoral, illegal intentions of abducting, molesting, and raping us! Those men had a real, powerful, and supernatural encounter with Warrior Angels! They had their EYES OPENED Into The Supernatural World!

I didn't have natural weapons, but I did have my faith, a real relationship with God and his Son Jesus Christ, and spiritual weapons of warfare! God delivered us with his mighty hand that night! I don't want to think of what would have happened if I had not used the only defense I had, which was a belief that God could and would protect us! Standing on my faith and verbally making that powerful proclamation that God would do just that, changed the entire situation! In fact, God saved us from rape and possibly death because many times perpetrators of rape will try to cover up that horrible crime by killing their victims.

Sherryl and I were extremely relieved when the men left. I shared with her the demonstrated power of God that we had just witnessed. It was an awesome, modern-day miraculous move of God!

We were two eighteen-year-old petite, female college students who could have disappeared forever if God had not been on our side! God truly, supernaturally delivered us! Glory be to the Name of the Lord!

Within about five minutes after the wicked men who threatened rape drove away, three other students, one male and two females walked in front of the administration building. They had the same idea about getting in line early and became the next students in the line. My friend and future roommate Sherryl, and I waited outside the rest of the night and we were the first in line to sign up for a dormitory suite with the full bathroom. Sherryl was the best roommate in the world; and we went on to enjoy a great year in college. I thank God that he protected us and that his will was for us to be safe and to continue to live our lives according to his divine will! I praise God for keeping us safe! God protected us and he can do the same for you in Jesus' name!

Words are Powerful

You do not have to submit to evil attacks from the devil! I encourage you to understand your rights as a child of God! Know the Scriptures! You have the authority to boldly rely on the Word of God, and verbally declare and stand on the outcome that you need, want, and deserve! We read in Romans 4:17,

"...Speak those things that be not as though they were." In other words, verbally declare or say your desired outcome, not what seems to be the inevitable. Once you declare or say something, believe in it and work toward the outcome that you confess. We know that according to James 2:20, "...Faith without works (or labor) is dead (or unproductive)." Your action should demonstrate your commitment to your goals and dreams!

There are scriptures that remind us that nothing happens until you say something! God created and established the world with his words! For example, in Genesis 1:3 God said, "Let there be light; and there was light." God could have simply thought about light and made it happen, but he spoke the Elohim (Creator God) words and it happened. I believe God did that to teach us a powerful principle of how pertinent it is to speak verbally to declare, create, confirm and empower manifestation of what we need and want to see in our lives and for those for whom we pray!

Proverbs 18:21 confirms this principle saying, "Death and life are in the power of the tongue; and you will live by the fruit thereby." In other words, if you speak negatively, you invite bad things to follow. Conversely, as you speak positive and uplifting things, blessings will manifest. Speak what you want to see, believe it and work toward it. Be careful to speak life and positive outcomes over yourself, family members, business interest, ministry, etc. You can have what you say, in Jesus' name!

After verbally saying positive declarations and affirmations, work toward the desired results. As you diligently work on the desired goals, in due season or in God's time, your dreams will eventually manifest into wonderful finished products or outcomes! After you have declared a positive thing for your life, believe it! Feed your spirit with prayer, faith, confirming Scriptures that encourage you, and the diligent work that will make it happen! Your diligence in working on the dreams, combined with believing in them (your faith), will bring about the breakthrough! It takes your faith and you working to cause the shift from stagnancy to sufficiency and beyond!

Although you may experience some financial setbacks in life, it is not going to stay on a negative if you keep the faith and never give up. Stand on the scripture in John 10:10 where Jesus says, "The thief (devil) comes to steal, and to kill, and to destroy. I have come that they may have life, and that they may have it (life) more abundantly." In other words, Jesus does not come with selfish intent to take from you, but he adds to your life. Jesus wants your life to have more meaning, peace, purpose, joy, and prosperity! So, what is an abundant life?

An abundant life is one with peace in your soul and your mind, a healthy body and more than enough to take care of your financial needs. The Greek word for abundant in John 10:10 is "perisson" which means, "exceedingly, very highly, beyond measure, more, superfluous, and a quantity so abundant as to be considerably more than what one would expect or anticipate."

I was inspired with a revelation from God that some of you reading this will reach an even higher place or position of superabundance! That is where you have exceeded abundant living and have millions of dollars to effectively reach back to bless many people! Superabundance means, "exceedingly above or excessive in quantity or abundance." Those who reach this level have an obligation to seek God to understand his will, and the best ways to maximize the sharing or giving of financial support. Luke 12:48 says, "To whom much is given, much will be required." With this wisdom, we know we are responsible to use our time, talent, wealth, and knowledge to help our family as well as others.

Keep working on your goals and dreams. Believe God's Word and you will have a positive harvest of blessings! I encourage you to know God wants you to live a victorious and blessed life. Seek God for his will for you and stand in faith as God intentionally leads you into paths of abundant blessings, and for some people superabundance!

Chapter 4

In My House With Intruders

Prior to becoming an educator, serving, and positively influencing students in public schools, I had an illustrious career as a civil servant with the Federal Government, the Department of Defense (DOD) at both Fort McPherson and Fort Gillem in Metro-Atlanta, Georgia. While working for Second United States Army, at Fort Gillem, I provided customer service and computer software and hardware support to approximately 250 civil service employees, military officers and enlisted soldiers. I managed the entire computer automation training program, ensuring that the employees' training needs were met and that all the classes were full. I also personally taught various automation classes to active duty one, two and three-star army generals. I conducted training classes for other army officers, enlisted soldiers, and civilian employees for First United States Army and Second United States Army.

I was later promoted and worked for the Department of the Army, Criminal Investigation

Division (CID) and served as a Division Chief for the Information Management Division. While at CID, I supervised military officers and enlisted soldiers, including writing their Officer and Enlisted Evaluation Reports. Although active duty military members are usually supervised and rated by other senior military members, the Lieutenant Colonel trusted my leadership and made me the Division Chief. I provided automation and communications purchase recommendations to military colonels to ensure the efficient expenditure of federal funds. I also sat on budget advisory boards. My expertise was needed at 72 subordinate offices throughout the Southeast region of the United States. This included me traveling to conduct many automation and communications inspections at various military bases to ensure compliance with established United States Army Regulations. I interviewed professionals from all walks of life and wrote articles for the Army Sentinel Newspaper as well as commentary for other military newsletters.

As a federal employee, I frequently traveled from Washington D.C. to Los Angeles, California, and many states in-between for various conferences, training, and other official events. One day, I was scheduled to catch a flight out of Atlanta, Georgia. At the time, I lived within a ten-minute drive from the army base where I worked, and it took me only twenty minutes to drive to the airport. Usually, I took my suitcase with me when I left in the morning, storing it in my trunk when I was traveling, but this time I did not. I made the decision to leave it and come back for it before driving to Hartsfield-Jackson Atlanta International Airport.

That morning it was very hectic at work and it seemed that I could not get out of the office as early as I planned to ensure a relaxed ride to the airport. I did not want to rush. I finally left work and once I arrived in my home's corner-lot driveway, I jumped out of the car, raced up the walkway and skipped up the seven brick steps. As I raised the keychain to unlock the door, twisted the key and stepped over the threshold, God audibly spoke to me saying, "You're not in here alone." I whispered back in a questioning voice, "I'm not in here alone?" Mine was a statement in a questioning way. God's warning did not make any sense to me because there was no obvious indication that our home was compromised and that it had been invaded! Since I was rushing to grab my suitcase and leave for the airport, I brushed aside the warning from the Lord. (Of course, I have spiritually matured now, and I would never do that again!)

As I walked down the hallway passing the guest bathroom, I glanced into the small room and thought to myself, 'It looks like somebody is in there.' Remarkably, I did not say this out loud, nor did I turn on the light to check the room.

EYES OPENED Into The Supernatural World!

I proceeded to my master bedroom where I heard a noise like someone's slight movement in my closet. I paused, listened, frowned with concern, but I kept walking towards my master room bathroom. I sat to use the restroom, but then I had an overwhelming impression in my spirit that someone was behind the shower curtain! I reached out my hand to pull it back, but I got a sudden, cautionary check in my spirit. I decided not to pull back the curtain to see if someone was there, which does not make any sense if you are really, alone! I quickly finished my personal business and washed my hands.

I grabbed my packed suitcase that was on the floor and walked rapidly back through the hallway, down the steps and out of the front door. I drove away not knowing what I would later find out. I was in my house with intruders!

* * *

I arrived at the airport and flew across the country for an official Temporary Duty (TDY) trip for the Department of the Army. I had a great and productive four days and returned to Georgia. When I got home, my husband (at the time) sat me down and said, "Permetrice, I have some bad news."

"Bad news? What's wrong?" I asked while I was standing up.

Permetrice Milroe Jackson

He stated, "The day you left to go TDY, somebody broke into the house."

"What? Someone broke into our home! Oh my God!" Suddenly, I felt very sick and immediately sat on the edge of the bed. Abruptly, memories from my departure date came flooding back to my mind and it was very overwhelming!

I reflected on the Lord's verbal warning to me as I stepped inside the house, "You're not in here alone," and all of the other subtle warnings such as the feelings and the "almost" interventions from that fateful day suddenly, came back to me. I realized that the perpetrators could have killed me, which is what sometimes happens when a homeowner interrupts a burglary. Since I walked in on their bold invasion into our home, had I seen their faces I would have been able to identify them, which probably would have made the men panic, attack and kill me.

Now, even though I was safe, and the incident was over, I felt over-whelming emotions of fear and anxiety of what could have happened. Unfortunately, a recent local news story came back to my mind in those few minutes as I processed what could have happened to me. One day the week before, a City of Atlanta employee had left work early because she felt sick. Unfortunately, she walked into her house during a burglary-in-progress and the perpetrators killed her. The terrible fear she must have experienced pained me at that moment. Nobody should have to endure such a hostile encounter. This poor victim and many more have died because criminals violate boundaries and break into homes to steal what they are too lazy to work and pay for. I thought about her then and her plight made me sad.

I also thought again about the audible voice of God saying to me before I even stepped fully into the house, "You're not in here alone." come back to me with precision. I thought about the feeling that I had when I thought I was passing somebody in the hall bathroom, but I did not stop, turn on the light and look. The memory of the noise that I heard from the master bedroom closet, yet I did not stop to investigate it, probably was one of the men. Finally, when I felt like someone was in my master bedroom bathroom behind the shower curtain: yet, I did not pull back the curtain, which I believe would have revealed one of the perpetrators. If anything had been different, I may have been face-to-face with violent criminals. While thinking of the horrible revelations of all that happened and how I was blessed to be saved from harm, I bowed my head and cried an ugly, shoulder-heaving up-and-down, meltdown of fear, relief and gratefulness to God for sparing my life! Mentally, it was a lot to process.

Since I did not actually see the perpetrators, you may be wondering how I am so certain about their existence and the number of men. Let me tell you...

Permetrice Milroe Jackson

* * *

A couple of days after I learned that our home had been invaded, I decided to visit an older couple, the Tuckers, who were my neighbors. Mrs. Tucker is a homemaker and Mr. Tucker was retired. During the visit, I told them about the issue that happened at our home. Mr. Tucker shared with me that he saw three young men leave my house right after I left. He assumed that I knew the young men since they left immediately after me; so, he did not call the police. He had no idea that they were fleeing criminals who probably thought I was going to get help.

Apparently, when I came in the house, the three perpetrators ran and hid in the hall bathroom, my master room closet and in the master bathroom shower. Since I came in the house and left out so quickly, it apparently startled them. I assume they thought I really did know they were in our home and that I was going to go get help or call the police.

We noticed that the thieves had broken the glass window in the day-basement and had entered the house by climbing through the window. They had gathered various electronics in the middle of the basement floor. We assume that they were upstairs figuring out what valuables they would steal from the bedrooms when they heard me come in. Fortunately, they did not take anything because no jewelry or other valuables were missing and the stash in the basement was still in the middle of the floor!

The Lesson Learned

This unfortunate incident could have ended tragically for me and I am grateful to God for his intervention! The main lesson I learned from this is to listen when I hear God's voice whether it is audible or the "still small voice" in my spirit. Since I heard God say, "You're not in here alone." when I was going in the house, I should have listened, stepped back out of the house, and called the police.

I thank God that he protected me despite my failure to listen to his warning. God chose to protect me in the middle of a very dangerous situation! We read in Psalms 3:2-3, "Many are saying of me, God will not deliver him, but you Lord, are a shield around me; my glory, and the lifter of my head." I Praise the Lord for his Divine protection!

5

Chapter 5

She Tried to Get Away

One evening as I exited the door of a shopping plaza where my husband had a store, the Spirit of God audibly said, "She hit your car!" I frowned and quickly proceeded to walk toward my vehicle that was far away from me, not visible from the door, and it was dark outside. I approached my car to see a woman who I knew was one of the shop owners, looking at the front of my car. She was parked in front of my vehicle. When the woman saw me approaching her, she pretended to search for something on the ground. Although she knew me, she did not speak to me, nor did she open her mouth to confess anything. She quickly turned away from me to get in her large white van!

Knowing what God had said to me as I left the building, by faith I said in a strong voice and affirmative manner, "Excuse me: You hit my car!" The woman looked stunned because she knew I was not out there, yet I had stated a fact, not asked her a question.

EYES OPENED Into The Supernatural World!

The woman knew she had hit my car and she assumed she was going to get away with the damage because she had quickly assessed the dent on my car and tried to deceive me by acting like she had dropped something once she glanced at me. With my firm exclamation, "You hit my car!" she was caught red-handed. Although she looked confused at how I could know she hit my car, she assumed that I saw the actual accident. Reluctantly, she confessed to hitting it. Ironically, she thought I knew because I witnessed the accident, but I only knew because God revealed it to me!

Remember, I did not actually see her do it, nor did I see the damage at that point, I just trusted God because he knew what she had done and he also knew that she intended to be deceitful and try to get away with it. If God had not told me the situation way before I approached the area, I would have leisurely walked to my car and she would have been gone.

This may seem like a little thing, but I was so thankful that the Lord revealed the information to me. I would not have had any way of knowing who damaged my car. I would have had a dented vehicle without any knowledge of who was responsible for the damage because the shopping plaza did not have video cameras.

Permetrice Milroe Jackson

I Have Learned to Listen...

Listen to God because he is awesome, all knowing, and kind enough to reveal pertinent things to us right on time! This reminds me of a Scripture in Proverbs 15:3 which says, "The eyes of the Lord are in every place, beholding the evil and the good." God sees and he knows everything! When God speaks or reveals something to you, LISTEN!

Chapter 6

Milton's Miracle Healing

Milton was a great family friend who was a blessing in many ways. When I went home to Chicago, Illinois to visit my family, he would come by and we would play board games, checkers, cards, and listen to good, old-school music! Milton would also take me out to dinner, or he would buy my favorite home-town foods and bring them to my mother's house for us to eat before game time. Some choices were the famous Chicago style barbeque ribs or rib tips and fries all drenched in BBQ sauce, deep-dish pizza, Vienna Beef Chicago Style hot dogs, fried fish dinners, grilled polish sausages smothered with grilled onions, and delicious Italian beef sandwiches simmered and served au jus on a long French Roll!

Unfortunately, Milton was very sick with a serious bowel blockage and he had been in a hospital for five days. He had been told that he would remain there indefinitely because the doctors and nurses had done all they could, and nothing had worked to relieve him of this serious condition.

Permetrice Milroe Jackson

Milton was in acute pain and the doctors ordered strong medication to help comfort him. Even if he slightly touched his stomach, he would wince in agony. I lived in a Georgia suburb, and my mother had called to tell me about his predicament. Although prayer has no distance limitation, I was very close to Milton; therefore, I wanted to fly home to visit him and pray for him in person.

I went home to Chicago with a priority to go visit Milton and lay hands on him the Bible way and pray for his miraculous healing. I was full of faith and I trusted God that if I would do like the Bible says in Mark 16:18, "...Lay hands on the sick and they shall recover..." that once I would do that, Milton would be healed of his painful condition.

My Mother and I walked in to see Milton and we enjoyed pleasant conversation. He told me how he could not use the restroom. He also touched his stomach and frowned with pain to demonstrate to me how much agony the issue was causing him.

I listened to Milton, but I wisely steered our conversation to the main reason that I was there. I shared with Milton the authority I had from God to lay hands on him to pray for his healing. Although Milton was not a born-again Christian at the time, he trusted the relationship that I had with the Lord Jesus because he really wanted to get well. Milton looked at me with respect as he joined his faith with mine for his healing.

EYES OPENED Into The Supernatural World!

I anointed Milton with olive oil that had been prayed over. I said, "Lord, you said I could pray for the sick and they would recover. Milton has been in this hospital for five days and his condition has not improved. Give the doctors and nurses the wisdom on how to treat him. I lay my hands on him now, and I command his bowels to MOVE in the name of Jesus! I thank you for healing Milton and turning his situation around in Jesus' name. Amen."

After I prayed for Milton, he still looked the same and he said he was in extreme pain. Although outwardly he had not changed, by faith I truly believed that God was going to heal him!

I encouraged Milton and concluded our visit with him. My Mother and I left to drive back to the South Side of Chicago. It took us almost one hour to get home because of the rush hour traffic.

When we walked into my mother's house, I placed my purse down and noticed that her landline telephone message indicator was blinking. She and I listened to a few messages, but we were amazed by one in particular!

Milton Taylor was my friend. Sometimes, he would playfully call me by my whole name, Permetrice Milroe Jackson, just to get me to smile. I smiled that day and I cried happy tears because Milton left an awesome message! The memory of it still warms my heart today.

Permetrice Milroe Jackson

Milton's phone message told a powerful story of the miracle-working power of a God that can still heal us today. At the time of this miracle, I was still working for the Federal Government, Department of the Army, traveling all over the United States visiting army bases where I conducted automation and communications inspections. Milton knew this, so he referenced my career in his message.

Milton said, "Permetrice Milroe Jackson, you need to stop traveling around the country fixing computers and start traveling around the country healing people! After you left out of my room, a nurse came in that I had never seen before. When she was ready to do my enema, I went to turn the way the other nurses told me to, but she told me to turn another way. Remember, you prayed for the doctors and nurses to have wisdom on how to care for me. Within thirty minutes, I felt a rumbling deep within me and all-of-a-sudden, my bowels moved! I messed up all-of my clothes and the entire bed, but I have never been so glad to use the bathroom! You healed me!!!" He started laughing. Needless-to-say, he was one happy, healed man!

Some people may think that Milton was better because of the enema. At that point, Milton had already been in the hospital for five days. The doctors were treating him and had ordered various medications, enemas, and the staff had run many tests and done other procedures, but nothing had worked!

Not one of the methods that the medical professionals tried was effective until I laid hands on him and prayed for his healing! I went "old-school" back to the Bible basics and God healed Milton!

I was ecstatic that Milton's healing manifested so quickly! Before I could drive across the city of Chicago to my Mother's house, God had healed him!

Of course, since Milton was giving me all the credit, I immediately called him and explained to him that I was just a vessel that the Lord Jesus used, but God was the healer! I will never try to steal God's glory or take credit for what God has done. I am just a minister that God uses to bless his people.

Some of you may be wondering why it took about thirty minutes for his healing to manifest. There is an example in the Bible where Jesus himself prayed for a man's servant and the Scripture says he was healed in the same hour. We see in Matthew 8:13, "Go your way; and as you have believed, so let it be done for you.' And his servant was healed that same hour."

In this scripture and with Milton, prayer and faith were activated to receive the desired result. Sometimes the natural body needs to catch hold of the anointed Word of God for the healing to manifest in the natural. After Milton had been sick at home for days and in the hospital for five days, once I prayed with him and we believed or had faith in the prayer and God's power and ability to heal him, within about thirty minutes, it happened! God truly moved and delivered Milton, giving him a miraculous healing!

Previously, the doctors had said Milton would be in the hospital indefinitely. After God touched his body and moved the bowel blockage, Milton was released the very next day! God moved for Milton and he can do the very same thing for you!

As Christians, we believe in science and the dedicated work of doctors and nurses. In fact, the Disciple Luke was a medical doctor. This assures us that it is wise to listen to doctors and follow their advice. Sometimes, the Lord allows people to go through a season of sickness and be treated by nurses and doctors. Other times just like in the Bible, there will be situations when the medical providers will do all they can do, but a miracle of healing is still needed. God can choose to intervene supernaturally!

To conclude, no matter what type of physical healing you need, God may use the doctors to help you get better. When necessary, sometimes people need a miracle. Know that God has the final say and he still has the power to heal you today, in the name of Jesus!

Chapter 7

Mansions in Heaven

As a child and even later, I often wondered what a Heavenly mansion would look like. Of course, like many of you, I have seen some beautiful mansions during my lifetime, and I celebrate the wonderful architectural skills of various builders. How do these designs compare to what is in store for Christian Believers in Heaven? In John 14:2-3, Jesus said, "In my father's house are many mansions: if it were not so, I would have told you. I go to prepare a place for you. And if I go and prepare a place for you, I will come again, and receive you unto myself; that where I am, there you may be also."

In John 14:2, the word "mansions" in the Greek is the word "meno" which means, "a staying, i.e. residence (the act or place); abode." It suggests a permanence of occupancy rather than being a temporary home. It implies stability. That is very comforting to me. I thank God for his assurance to us that as we walk with him on the earth, we have a relationship with him now, but we will also have wonderful rewards waiting for us in eternity. I hope that comforts you to know that God has made promises to you that will be wonderful to enjoy throughout eternity!

I Saw a Heavenly Mansion!

God allowed me to dream of a magnificent, Heavenly mansion! It was made of huge rectangular, equal sized slabs of spectacular fancy marble. The marble had a rich hue of deep mauve with elegant ivory vein patterns. There were windows, but no screens because there will be no irritating insects in Heaven! A brilliant light from God illuminated the entire mansion! This divine light was so bright that it also shone on the surrounding area outside of the house. Notably, there were no lamps or other physical lights anywhere because God is Light, and his presence supplied an abundance of brightness. We find in James 1:17, "Every good gift and every perfect gift is from the Father of Lights, with whom is no variableness, neither shadow of turning;" I also read this reference to God's light in Revelations 22:5 which says, "And there will no longer be any night there; and they will not have need of the light of a lamp nor the light of the sun, because the Lord God will illuminate them; and they will reign forever and ever."

Before approaching the Heavenly mansion, I saw the same beautiful marble made into an inviting walkway that seemed to beckon me. The walkway under my feet, was made of marble squares that measured about 14" x 14" inches, placed neatly together. On top of the walkway was beautiful, crystal clear water that was at least 12 inches deep, yet I never felt that my feet were wet. As I approached the entrance door of the mansion, I walked along the walkway, but since my feet were not wet, I guess I walked above or on the water because I approached the entrance to the impressive mansion with dry feet! I was curious about this crystal clear water so I studied the Bible and found context in Revelations 22:1, "Then he showed me a river of the water of life, clear as crystal, coming from the throne of God and of the Lamb, in the middle of its street."

Once I was at the grand door of the beautiful, Heavenly mansion, I assumed that I would be touring inside of it, but I abruptly woke up from this powerful, prophetic dream. I concluded that God wants me to wait to get my very own Heavenly mansion one day, to see all the other awesome details that I will enjoy throughout eternity!

In the Bible, 1 Corinthians 2:9 says, "But as it is written, Eye has not seen, nor ear heard, neither have entered into the heart of man, the things which

God has prepared for them that love him." In other words, there are treasures and rewards waiting for us that are so special that we cannot imagine their splendor. Live for the Lord; so that you will have peace in your soul now and forever. When we get to Heaven, we will enjoy all the tremendous, eternal blessings that God has prepared for us! Praise God!

Marvelous Marble

Marble is a beautiful stone that is used for sculptures, architectural buildings, pillars, furniture, and countertops. Calacatta marble is pretty and rare. It is only found in one quarry in Carrara, Italy, so its supply is limited. The most expensive marble in the world is Lux Touch Marble which sells for one million dollars per square meter! It is truly gorgeous, but the marble that I saw on the Heavenly mansion was more spectacular than I have ever seen in this world! That mansion was majestic and spiritual, reserved for God's children who willingly choose to serve him and accept Jesus as their Savior. Heaven's magnificence makes me want to shout for joy!

Chapter 8

Hell Is Real!

In Heaven, Lucifer was over praise and worship. He had status, but he allowed his position to make him arrogant and full of pride! He decided that he was great enough to be equal with God and he rebelled against God: therefore, he was expelled or thrown out of Heaven! His angels were cast out of Heaven with him according to Revelation 12:9, "And the great dragon was case out, that old serpent, called the Devil and Satan, which deceives the whole world: he was cast out into the earth, and his angels were cast out with him."

We see that the name Lucifer is written in Isaiah 14:12, where he is admonished, "How are thou fallen from Heaven, O Lucifer, son of the morning." The Hebrew word translated "Lucifer" means "shining one." Lucifer was special and highly favored until he decided to rebel and defy God.

The Bible says in 1 Peter 5:8, "Be sober, be vigilant; because your adversary the devil, as a roaring lion, walks about, seeking whom he may devour." In other words, the devil is not your friend and he has the insatiable desire to harm you.

Since the devil lost his position and was thrown out of Heaven, he is angry with God and his people who choose to follow God's principles. He does not want you to go to the magnificent place called Heaven where he once lived. He hates you and fights against you because he wants you to miss this eternal place of peace, love, rest, joy, and eternal fellowship with the Living God.

Hell is a real place that was created by God for Lucifer and the fallen angels who were cast out of Heaven. It is a place of torment and misery. In Luke 13:28, we find, "There will be weeping and gnashing of teeth." Crying and gnashing of teeth or grinding down in pain, anguish, or anger; does not sound like a place where you would want to be.

I realize some people trivialize the reality of a literal place called Hell. Some singers and rappers have tried to place a glamorous spin on Hell like it is a place to party and have a good time. The devil uses this horrible strategy to deceive people so that they will not fear an eternal destiny of death, demonic torment, decay, hot burning flames, and misery throughout eternity. I realize this chapter of the book is not something to shout about or make you happy, but you need to understand that Hell is Real! God allowed me to have a glimpse of Hell and I assure; you do not want to go there!

EYES OPENED Into The Supernatural World!

My Visit to Hell

I dreamed that I visited Hell! The Lord allowed me to observe and be aware, without feeling the consequence or torment of those suffering there. I could hear the screams of the lost souls who were tortured in that horrible pit! Specifically, in the dream I saw two African American young men with bandanas around their heads. In their young lives, they had been friends and fellow gang members. While in the dream, the Lord let me know that they unfortunately, had been involved in a gun shootout and tragically killed.

Now in Hell, the young men who had once been close friends were arguing, blaming each other because they had ended up in that horrible place! The young men were suffering in agonizing flames and demonic spirits gleefully tortured them. The demons also afflicted others who were trapped in the various rooms and walls of Hell. The rooms looked like dark, gloomy and eerie jail cells with the faces of suffering, petrified souls.

After seeing these horrific scenes, I continued to walk further while hearing the frantic screams of tormented people whose pleading eyes and flailing arms begged for my help. Of course, there was nothing I could do for them. I walked away feeling grieved for the young men and the others who were suffering.

Permetrice Milroe Jackson

In the same dream, I saw an elderly white woman smiling while sitting in a rocking chair, moving back and forth. She looked like a kind old woman and in my mind; I wondered why she was in Hell. At first, she looked amused, as she grinned, but within seconds, her beaming countenance turned into an ugly frown as screams of terror and agony escaped her lips. The change was so fast that I was shocked, but within seconds I saw the source of her pain.

I had been focused on the elderly woman's smiling face, but as I continued to watch her, I suddenly noticed the flames blazing up from under her rocking chair coming up and around her causing her to yell in anguish! I could feel the heat of the fire, but not the impact of the flames. In other words, I was not burning, but I felt the heat from the flame that was scorching her! It was an intense heat and I felt sad for her; yet there was nothing that I could do to help her. She was obviously miserable: being burned and tormented by the fire.

Immediately, I felt compassion and I worried for a few seconds. The Lord Jesus let me know that the woman had refused to repent of her sins and accept him as her Savior. Not only did she reject salvation through the blood of Jesus, the woman harbored hatred in her heart toward African Americans or Black people. She was a racist woman and during her lifetime on earth, she had mistreated people of color. I walked away from her feeling sad for her soul that was forever, eternally, lost.

Two Scenes in Hell

These two accounts from the pit of Hell may seem unbelievable, but they are what God showed me. Hell is a real place, where real people spend a real eternity! Please do not ignore this warning! Repent of your sins and accept Jesus as your Lord and Savior. Eternity is too long, and Hell is too hot to gamble with your soul! God will not show mercy to the souls that choose to go to Hell because he has made the provision for you while you are living to accept his Son Jesus Christ, as your Savior. Please repent of your sins and get saved, so that you will go to Heaven instead of Hell. Remember, it is your choice!

Once in Hell, there is no way out! It is a torturous sentence for all eternity! Again, it is your choice, but I encourage you to choose wisely. The Bible says in Joshua 24:15, "...Choose you this day, who you will serve." I beg you to get your life in order and choose the Lord Jesus as your Savior. It would be the best decision of your life!

Unfortunately, for people who refuse God's Plan of Salvation, Hell can house an unlimited number of souls throughout eternity. The Bible says in Isaiah 5:14, "Therefore Hell has enlarged herself, and opened her mouth without measure: and their glory, and their multitude, and their pomp (or arrogance), and he that sins (habitually, without repenting and accepting Jesus), shall descend into it (Hell)."

Demonic Influence

Have you ever wondered what makes people commit evil acts against humanity? The devil and his demons influence people to perpetrate atrocious crimes. For example, before committing a horrible crime, a mass shooting suspect made a dangerous, disastrous declaration on his Facebook page saying, "I am about to go to Hell and I'm not coming back!"

This was a very sad, negative, and morbid pronouncement of his own eternal fate. He made the decision to kill innocent people, shooting and killing nine individuals! He injured 26 others while using an assault style, automatic weapon. While actively engaging in this egregious crime, police officers shot and killed him. The officers were in the same area of the tragedy and therefore responded within 31 seconds of the panicked 911 calls. This man said he was going to Hell. He murdered people and he was killed by policemen while actively trying to shoot and kill more people.

God allowed me to see parts of Hell and from that observation, I know it is a horrific place that you would not want to be for even one second, much less for all eternity! God made Hell as a punishment for Satan and his fallen angels. Hell is a real, physical place and I promise - you do not want to go there! There will be no escaping the fire, stench, demonic torment, darkness, despair, and all things miserable in Hell. I plead with you to make the choice to repent or turn away from your sins; accept the Lord Jesus as your Savior and develop a relationship with him.

You can grow or mature in God through daily prayer or communication, loving him and your neighbors, learning about the Holy Scriptures by attending a Bible believing church and being obedient to his Word and his Will for your life. Giving my life to the Lord Jesus Christ as a sixteen-year-old high school student was the absolute best decision that I have ever made. That wise choice has positively impacted my entire life! God loves you! He will forgive you of your sins, welcome you into the Family of God, and help you grow up spiritually!

Chapter 9

Devilish Details…Demons

There was an angel in Heaven who was responsible for praise and worship. He was the highest-ranking angel, but he was unsatisfied with that. His name was Lucifer, which in Latin means, "light bearer, shining one and morning star" which indicates that he was given gifts to lead. His name was changed to Satan, which in the Hebrew means "adversary" which implies that he is against you as a child of God. Though Lucifer was beautiful and had a melodious voice, unfortunately, he became filled with pride and decided that he would ascend and be like God or even higher than God. In Ezekiel 28:17, the Bible says, "Your heart became proud on account of your beauty, and you corrupted your wisdom because of your splendor." What? Yes. It was absurd for Lucifer to think that a created being could ever become greater than the All Mighty God who created him, but that is what he thought. The Bible says in Isaiah 14:12-14, "How you are fallen from Heaven, O Lucifer, son of the morning! …For you have said in your heart: 'I will ascend into Heaven, I will exalt my throne above the stars of God; I will also sit enthroned on the mount of the congregation on the farthest sides of the North; I will ascend above the heights of the clouds, I will be like the Most High." Because of his pride and sin, God cast Lucifer out of Heaven and there were fallen angels who were also cast out.

The earliest mention of Satan is recorded in Genesis Chapter 3 when he influenced the serpent to tempt Eve to eat of the forbidden fruit from the Tree of the Knowledge of Good and Evil. She and her husband Adam yielded to the temptation and ate of the fruit, which led to the fall of man.

In Genesis Chapter 4:1-18, we read where Cain was influenced by the devil and committed the first murder when he killed his brother Abel. Cain was jealous of Abel's obedient sacrifice that God was pleased with, whereas God was not pleased with Cain's offering. At that time, the offerings were to include a blood sacrifice of their best animals and although Cain knew this, he presented fruits and vegetables in an act of disobedience and rebellion.

Unfortunately, this first act of murder has been followed by a spirit of murder in many urban cities and rural towns in America and around the world. There have been too many mass shootings resulting in many injuries and deaths. This is very disturbing. These brutal acts of violence are not committed by people with the love of God in their hearts: but people filled with hatred and influenced by demonic spirits.

In the New Testament, devil (diabolos) means "false accuser, Satan, slanderer" in the Greek and is the word from which the English word diabolical is formed. In Revelation 12:9 and in Revelation 20:2, Satan is called a dragon and that old serpent; and Matthew 4:3 calls him the "tempter" of men. Other names for the devil include Abaddon, which means "destruction," and Apollyon, which translates to or means "destroyer." All these names and meanings imply that the devil or Satan is not a "being" that means you any good, but he wants to harm you. I wanted to give some information and scriptures reference to the devil and demons to bring clarity and understanding that they do exist.

Jesus said in John 10:10, "The thief (devil) comes only to steal, kill and to destroy; I am come that they might have life, and that they might have it more abundantly."

No matter what trials I encounter, I always believe for the better or the abundant life that Jesus has promised me. If things are going wrong for you right now, God is not finished. He will turn things around for you. Just trust him and his process. If you stay with God, everything is going to work out for your ultimate good.

Love God and Get the Good

There is a principle of God allowing every situation that you find yourself in or going through to ultimately work for your good. This assurance is found in Romans 8:28; "And we know that **all** things work together for **good** to them that love God, to them who are the called according to his purpose." God knows how to let us come through a negative situation and come out better than we were before. We can learn from our bitter trials, grow spiritually, and become wiser in the process. As we learn and grow, we become a living testimony for those times when we meet somebody going through a similar circumstance. When this happens, we can empathize with others and sincerely encourage and help them make it through their difficult circumstances.

Bad things happen, but God is still in control.

The negative things that occur in the world today such as people physically attacked, horrible mass shootings, murders, physical, verbal, or sexual abuse, assaults, armed robberies, as well as an array of other crimes against humanity are committed too often. Demonic beings behind the scenes, in the unseen world, influence these occurrences.

We can agree that a loving God would not encourage people to commit such atrocities. We have already covered John 10:10 which says, "The thief (devil) comes to kill, steal and destroy. I came that they may have life and have it (life) more abundantly." It is safe to say that the devil is the influence behind individuals who commit these crimes.

Some people think individuals with mental health issues are the main perpetrators of crimes. According to a study by the American Psychological Association (APA), "Crimes committed by people with serious mental disorders, only 7.5 percent were directly related to symptoms of mental illness. The study didn't find any predictable patterns linking criminal conduct and mental illness symptoms over time. The lead researcher, Dr. Jillian Peterson stated, "The vast majority of people with mental illness are not violent, not criminal and not dangerous." The study was published online in the APA Journal, "Law and Human Behavior."

Some people diagnosed with an official mental health diagnoses may hurt themselves due to depression, schizophrenia disorder (hallucinations and delusions) or bi-polar disorder (impulsivity and risk-taking behavior). They normally do not hurt other people. They need the mental health treatment or medication and access to therapy and counseling to mentally heal, improve, recover, and thrive.

I submit to you that many of the crimes in society today against innocent people are committed because people choose to connect with hate groups and hateful ideology. Many mass murderers connect with other hateful people who think and feel like they do to justify their horrible thoughts and heinous acts. I believe hatred is behind these crimes against others. It is sad, but there are too many examples of violence and hateful acts against innocent people around the world.

God is love; therefore, hate comes from the devil! We must not allow the enemy of our soul, the devil, to come into us and cause us to hate our neighbors or anyone else just because they look differently from us. We are all on earth together and we must learn how to get along.

I Saw a Demon

It seemed like a normal evening where I assumed that I would rest until the time of my alarm clock beckoning me to "rise and shine" for the day. I went to sleep…

Permetrice Milroe Jackson

As I slept, I started dreaming that I was walking outside in a meadow. I felt at peace for a while, but suddenly I felt a wicked presence around me. I looked back and saw a horrible looking demon behind me, chasing me. I started running until I fell face down. I decided to roll onto my back. Once on my back, I woke up and realized that I was in my own bedroom. I looked around and saw my furniture. Suddenly, I realized that the evil, demon spirit was on top of my chest trying to crush me! What was I going to do?

I felt like the very life was leaving my body. I tried to say 'Stop,' but nothing came out of my lips. I couldn't move or say anything. I tried to push the demon spirit off me, but I did not have the strength to lift it from my chest. I tried to speak in-order-to get my husband's attention, but I could not verbally say anything because the demonic spirit had its filthy hands over my mouth and my nose, trying to suffocate me! I tried to say other words to command the demon to get off me because I could not breathe! At last, in a moment of desperation, I had the presence of mind to call on the name of the Lord Jesus!

Suddenly, I literally screamed to the top of my lungs, "Jesus!" Instantly, the demon spirit released me. As I previously mentioned, I was wide-awake; but ironically, I was not afraid. I glanced at my husband who appeared to be asleep. I decided to follow suit and I turned over and went back to sleep, totally at peace. Isn't that amazing that the Lord allowed me to feel no fear? I felt peaceful once the demon spirit was gone. I thank God that he is a very present help in the time of a storm, trouble, or any attack from the devil!

The Next Morning...

The next morning, I woke up feeling perfectly fine, but as I was getting ready to go to work, God brought the dream, me waking up and the demonic attack, back to my mind.

I mentioned to my husband that a demon spirit had attacked me the night before. Guess what he mentioned to me. He said, "Permetrice, in the middle of the night, you screamed out 'Jesus!' and it was loud enough to wake me up!" (He was a sound sleeper.) He further stated, "I woke up because you screamed so loudly. You sat up in the bed, looked around and then you laid back down and went right back to sleep." His account confirmed mine.

Permetrice Milroe Jackson

That Demon Sure Was Ugly!

The demonic spirit that tried to take my life by resting its heavy weight on my chest and covering my mouth and nose was massive in size. It was approximately five feet wide. I cannot estimate its height because I saw it while I was in a horizontal posture while in my bed. The demon had facial features like humans, but they were horrifying and grotesque which I assume is because they are evil. It may also be because they want to strike fear in those for whom they appear or attack. Unlike the angels' white robes that were flowing and pretty that I had previously witnessed and explicitly described in another chapter, the demon's garment was a mixture of smoky grey and brown. The material looked old, rough, tattered, and very soiled. The demonic spirit seemed to float appearing weightless, but this was deceptive because when it pounced onto my chest area, its weight was extremely heavy, and it felt overwhelming. Its intention was to kill me through suffocation, but God did not allow it to succeed. The Lord Jesus gave me the victory!

The heavy weight of the demon's mass reminds me of how loaded down people are as they choose to practice habitual sin. Although you may feel as though you are having a great time, doing whatever you feel like doing as a "grown" person; know that sin has a debt to pay and the fun for a season, is

EYES OPENED Into The Supernatural World!

deceptive. Romans 6:23 says, "For the wages of sin is death, but the gift of God is eternal life through Jesus Christ our Lord."

Your soul is too valuable to take a chance on making a deathbed confession to accept Jesus Christ as your Savior. You do not know how you will die or when it will happen. It would be better to live for God, accept his Son Jesus as your Savior and live throughout eternity in peace! Please consider your precious soul and surrender to the Lord Jesus Christ!

Chapter 10

God and the Pole

I was born and raised in Chicago, Illinois which is known for having a very diverse population, delicious foods, wonderful museums, multiple major league sports teams, cold winter weather, and the beautiful Lake Michigan, just to name some of its features. It was during one of the cold winter days that I had an unfortunate incident on the traffic-filled Dan Ryan Expressway.

I was driving from my Mother's home to my aunt's house one evening before it was dark. I did not see what I later determined to be black ice on the lanes. Suddenly, my car started sliding and I went into an uncontrollable spin in the middle of the Dan Ryan Expressway! If you are familiar with this highway, you know it is always densely occupied. One spin across those busy lanes could be certain death. That day, it was as if God had the cars stand still because I did not see any cars driving toward me! My car rotated once, twice and when I went into the beginning of the third rotation, my eyes were staring at a pending, metal light pole directly next to my face! It was literally seconds, and only inches from me! There was absolutely nothing I could do to move the pole; or no humanly possible method to avoid hitting it! I braced for the impact to my face and head, putting my left hand up as a shield while holding the steering wheel with my right hand. My car was now turned facing the opposite way partly in the emergency lane and in the grass. It happened so fast that I did not have time for a long prayer for my safety and deliverance. In that split second, all I could do was scream, "Jesus!"

My car came to an abrupt halt WITHOUT hitting the pole! This was humanly impossible. I opened my eyes with scrunched up brows because remember, that pole was close enough for me to impulsively shield my face with my left hand. In that moment, I wanted to know how it was possible to avoid bashing my head into the cold metal. As I opened my eyes and blinked, confused, shaking my head in stunned disbelief because I knew hitting that structure would have been horrible and possibly fatal!

Once my eyes popped open, I saw the clear hilly lawn that lines the expressway through my driver's side window, but I didn't see the giant pole that only seconds before had been near my face! I quickly turned my head to look at the passenger door. Although the car did not spin again, the pole was on the right side of the car next to the passenger door! I do not know if God or an angel moved the pole or picked the car up and miraculously, simultaneously placed it back down in that "split" second. All I know is it was a modern-day miracle and I lived to tell about it! As I proofread this section, I teared up because the experience was so profound! God spared my life that day and I am truly grateful!

The plot the devil had written was to seriously harm me, or for me to die a premature death. God changed my situation and saved me from the accident that had tragedy written all over it! It was not my time to leave this earth! God delivered me once again! He knew I had a full, intentional life to live, children to raise, destiny to fulfill, powerful sermons to preach, and novels and inspirational books to write. I Praise God for his mighty and miraculous interventions that have saved my life! Know that he can do the very same for you if you believe in, love, and live for him! Hallelujah!

Chapter 11

A Dream to Bring Comfort

My husband was driving on the expressway when he witnessed a tragic accident between an eighteen-wheeler and an automobile. Our four-year old daughter Jaleese was with him. He pulled over to the emergency lane and exited our car while holding her. He walked up to the vehicle to see a young man badly injured, but still conscience and breathing. The victim was in obvious pain. He placed his hand on the young man's shoulder to try to comfort him saying, "It's going to be okay." He also prayed for the young man and encouraged him to give his life to the Lord Jesus Christ. He decided to stay with the victim until the ambulance arrived.

Once the help came, one of the Emergency Medical Technicians made him move out of the way. They removed the young man from the car, placed him on a gurney, treated him, put him in the ambulance and transported him to the hospital.

When my husband and daughter got home, they shared what they saw. My daughter was extremely traumatized because she not only saw the massive amount of blood at the scene, but she described the broken bone that protruded from the young man's arm.

The accident was so bad that it made the local news, although they didn't show a picture of the victim. Unfortunately, we found out later that the young man did not survive the traumatic accident. He died at nineteen years old.

Since I was not there, the only thing that I knew about the young man was that he was African American. It disturbed me that he died so young, especially because I have a son. I also had the dilemma of comforting my daughter who had seen the sad and disturbing image of the accident victim. Even though we did not know him, we were saddened by his death.

I went to sleep a couple nights after the accident and dreamed about the teenager who was tragically killed. I saw him in a vivid dream, very happy and smiling. He was sitting on a sofa, playing with an infant, baby girl who was laughing at him. The child looked to be about two to three months old. It was obvious that both the young man and the baby were familiar with each other as he sat and played with her. I felt a wonderful sense of peace in the dream as I watched their interaction. I wondered whether the baby girl was his daughter or what the relationship was since he clearly loved her. The Lord let me know that the young man was at peace with God.

EYES OPENED Into The Supernatural World!

Of course, I wanted to give the parents and the family of the young man some comfort in the mist of their horrible time of bereavement. I did not know how I would be able to reach them, but God had a plan.

"It's a small world," someone once said. Coincidentally, somebody that we knew was an associate of the family of the young man. I asked if they would call the parents to see if they would allow me to talk to them. The mother agreed that I could have her number and I was told that she looked forward to talking with me.

* * *

I really wanted to be a blessing to the mother of the young man killed in the horrendous accident, so I prayed before calling her. Naturally, she was grief stricken, but she also was comforted to hear that her son was not alone during that traumatic time because I explained to her that my husband had stayed with him, encouraged him and prayed for him before the police and the medical help arrived.

After giving my condolences to the mother for the loss of her son, I described the vivid dream that God had allowed me to have. I told her that I saw her son smiling and happy, sitting on a sofa playing with an infant baby girl. The mother laughed in the mist of her tears when I described the scene to her. She stated that her son had a brand new three-month-old niece for whom he truly loved. She took all the information that I shared with her as a revelation from God that her son was at peace in Heaven. She knew that I had no way of knowing about his sweet little niece whom he loved, but God knew it.

God is so good to use me, or any of his servants, to see in the Spirit realm and give words of prophetic knowledge and wisdom to encourage others. In this situation, God gave me a detailed dream to help bring comfort to a grieving family. I Praise God for using me to console them.

Chapter 12

God Put Me in Their Business

This will be a very brief story of how God can get somebody's attention just to say, "I am God and I can do what I want to do, when I want to do it!"

I use a credit union for some of my financial business. There was a head-teller there who I often conducted my transactions with because she was so professional and personable. Let me just preface this by saying that I never thought about her when I was home, so this occurrence is even more amazing because there is no correlation as to why God put me in her business.

I had a dream about this teller who usually waited on me at the credit union. In the dream, I saw her sitting at a table with her husband who I had never met, but in the dream, I knew it was her husband. Although they looked busy conducting business, I walked toward them, stopping two feet from the table. She noticed me and stopped talking to her husband and another man who was their lawyer.

In the dream, the teller beckoned me closer to see a check she had just written. I looked at the substantial amount of the check. That is all that I saw, and I slept peacefully the rest of the night.

The next morning, I thought about the dream concerning the woman, her husband, the lawyer, and the large amount of the check. Two days later, I went to the credit union not really knowing how I would bring up the subject matter with her because we were not social friends.

I decided to approach the teller and ask a simple question. After her normal pleasantries and my reply, I said, "Let me ask you a question. Are you about to make a large purchase?"

She answered, "No. Why do you ask?"

I said, "This might sound strange, but I had a dream about you. I saw you and your husband sitting at a table with a lawyer and you had written a large check." I proceeded to tell her the amount of the check that I saw in the dream.

She sat back in her stool, smiled in disbelief and said, "I don't believe this! When you asked me if I was about to make a large purchase, I knew I was not buying anything big, so I said no. You may not believe this, but my husband and I just wrote a check for the exact amount that you said, for a down payment on a house for our son and daughter-in-law. I cannot believe that you dreamed that!" She was absolutely amazed that God would show me something that personal and accurate as the exact amount of the check she had written.

All I could say was that the Lord showed me; and I congratulated her on the fact that she and her husband were able to help their son and daughter-in-law achieve the American dream of owning a home. I Praise God that he truly can do whatever he wants to do when he wants to do it! Giving me that detailed dream was just a demonstration of his ability to show his servants things that are humanly impossible for them to know on their own. Our God is Awesome! I thank God for Divine Revelation Knowledge and supernatural, Spiritual Dreams!

Chapter 13

Holy Ghost Power and Purpose

As I wrote portions of this book, I could feel the power and the fire of the Holy Ghost, which is the Spirit of God. The Lord let me know that I needed to include a chapter about the Holy Spirit.

The Holy Ghost is one part of the Trinity: God the Father, the Son Jesus Christ, and the Holy Ghost. The three are one according to 1 John 5:7 "...For there are three that bear witness in Heaven, the Father, The Word (Jesus, the Son of God) and the Holy Ghost: and these three are one." These three are one and therefore they agree with each other.

The purpose of the Holy Ghost is to lead, guide, comfort, protect and reveal God's will for you in the earth. Have you ever been going someplace, and you suddenly feel an intense "warning" in your spirit not to go? Then you find out later that there was a big fight, an accident, or some other negative incident, at the very time that you had planned to be there? That was the Spirit of God warning you. It is up to you to listen and to obey that gentle leading of the Spirit of God.

Holy Ghost Comforter

Jesus said that he would go away, but he would leave help for us in the earth. In John 14:16, Jesus said, "And I will pray the Father, and he shall give you another Comforter (Helper), that he may abide with you forever." In times of loneliness, stress, suffering, adversity, heartbreak, betrayal, illness, bereavement or pain of any kind, the Holy Ghost will comfort you and help you through your trials, if you lean on and trust God. You do not have to suffer alone. Call on the Lord; he will answer your prayers! Remember, God knows what is best for you and he really does love and care about you!

The Holy Ghost Warns Us

I was walking in my home one day and suddenly, I saw in the Spirit a vision of a car accident. It was so strong, and I knew it involved me or one of my daughters. I immediately started praying about it, hoping that I could intervene and prevent the accident from happening. I spoke to my daughters and told them to be very careful driving that week. I didn't mention the vision, but I wanted to warn them to be extra cautious while traveling around the city.

Two days after I saw the vision of the car accident, I received a call from my older daughter. She stated that she was on her way to work, driving straight on a two-lane highway and a woman who was driving on the opposite side suddenly turned in front of her, hitting my daughter! The impact was so hard that my daughter's wig flew off her head! The car my daughter was driving was totaled. The wayward driver not only hit my daughter, but another car as well.

I shared the vision that I had with her and she was amazed. In my prayer time, I had asked God to shield and protect me and my daughters and of course, I had hoped an accident would not happen. Sometimes we have a bad experience in life, but I am very thankful that her life was spared. If you could have seen the damage to the car, you would have thought somebody may have died in the wreck and as I stated, the car was totaled. I am thankful that the Lord blessed my daughter with just minimal injuries, bruises, and soreness. She needed medical attention and physical therapy, but she survived.

When God shows you something, it is for a purpose and you should seek his face in prayer.

EYES OPENED Into The Supernatural World!

Although some negative situations occur in our lives, God's power can decrease the severity and he can bless you and your love ones to make it through the calamity in a victorious way!

* * *

Another time years ago, I was sitting at my desk working and I saw a vision of my husband in a car collision. I looked at the clock to note the time. It was 10:31a.m. I immediately started praying for him, rebuking the accident, and I asked God to let angels surround the car and protect him. In about thirty minutes, I called him. I told him that I saw a vision of him in a bad accident, I rebuked it, and prayed for his protection, and I wanted to check to see if he was okay. He was shocked that I saw it supernaturally and told me that a large truck was heading toward him in what would have been a horrible head-on collision that morning, but by a miracle, the truck didn't hit him! He asked me what time I had the vision. I told him that I had the vision and prayed for him at 10:31a.m. He was stunned and said that the near tragic accident happened at that exact time! That is amazing! I thank God for using me to intervene in prayer for his safely. Our God is an on-time God! He is awesome in all his ways!

Permetrice Milroe Jackson

The Holy Ghost Reveals God's Will

The Holy Ghost is a revealer of things, places, resources, and a situation solver if you will only pray and listen to his "still, small voice," as the old folks would say. God knows how to speak to his people. Though rare, God may speak to you audibly or out loud. I have heard him speak audibly and it is a special and extraordinary occurrence. Though God may choose to speak audibly, he usually speaks through his Word, the Holy Bible, by leading you to read particular Scriptures that will address your current need. He also speaks through his servants such as pastors, evangelists, prophets, and preachers as they deliver eloquent and anointed sermons. Finally, God can use other true servants or saints of God who are full of wisdom who can bless you with Godly advice.

Keep Personal Information Private

If God chooses to use you to reveal some information to an individual, take the task or assignment seriously and do not divulge or tell anyone else for whom the Lord has not authorized you to share the personal information. God's business is serious; and the person's personal business must be respected, especially if it is confidential!

The Holy Ghost Gives You Power

Once you submit your life and will to God, his Son Jesus Christ and the Spirit of God, you are not walking in this world by yourself. The seed of the Lord Jesus is planted in your soul and spirit and the seed grows as you apply the Christian principles and allow the Holy Ghost to work in your everyday life. You have the power to live right through the Holy Ghost. The Bible says in Acts. 1:8 "But ye shall receive power, after that the Holy Ghost is come upon you: and ye shall be witnesses unto me both in Jerusalem and in all Judaea, and in Samaria, and unto the uttermost part of the earth." In other words, wherever you live and wherever you go, the Spirit of God gives you the Power or Authority to accomplish the purposes of God for your life.

The word Power in Acts 1:8 is the Greek word Dynamis or Doo'-nam-is which means force (literally or figuratively); especially miraculous power (usually by implication, a miracle itself); ability, abundance, meaning mighty deeds, worker of miracles(s), strength, or wonderful work. This word is where we get the word dynamite, and we know the power in that substance! I listed all of the meanings for Power or Dynamis/Doonamis to inform you that you are a powerful force with the Lord's Spirit working through you! Hallelujah to God!

Chapter 14

God Knew About the Red Truck

When my son was five years old, there was a convenience store that I frequently used near my former home. On the right side of the building, there was a parking lot. On the left side, there was a huge, dumpster that blocked the left side of the building. If you drove to the back of the store from the right side, you were forced to come back out on the right side where the parking spaces were because of the dumpster that permanently blocked the left side.

One day my son and I were leaving the store as we had done so many times before. As we walked along the front of the store on the walkway in the direction to where I had parked my car, my son ran ahead of me. Suddenly, in my mind, I saw a vision of a moving, red vehicle "flash before me" on the left side of the building! This made no sense to me because I knew the dumpster was on that side of the building, blocking access like it had always done for many years. I did not have time to rationalize what I saw in the Spirit realm or argue with the Holy Ghost!

That split-second vision, of a "flash of a moving red vehicle" indicated that my son who had run out in front of me was in imminent danger! He was about to step off the store's walkway onto the pavement in front of where the dumpster was!

By faith, I immediately screamed at my son, "Stop, Roger!" As I previously stated, this made no sense to my natural mind, but I knew what the Lord had just shown me. My son had never heard me scream at him like that! It frightened him; therefore, he suddenly stopped walking just seconds before stepping off the store's walkway onto the pavement.

As soon as my son stopped, a bright red pick-up truck sped from around the corner where the dumpster had always been! I gasped for breath as I realized that my son would have been hit and killed. If I had not listened to, and immediately obeyed God's supernatural, revelation knowledge warning of the vision of the moving red vehicle that "flashed through my mind" in that split second, it would have been a tragedy! I had no idea the dumpster that had blocked that side of the building for years; had been moved and now both sides of the building had a lane for traffic flow. I did not know, but the Spirit of God, the Holy Ghost knew! I was so relieved that I grabbed my son, held him tight and cried happy tears as I Praised the God that I love and his Spirit, the Holy Ghost that revealed the danger that I could not see! Bless the Name of the Lord!

EYES OPENED Into The Supernatural World!

This lets us know that just like the red truck that I could not see and did not know about, posed an imminent threat to my son's life, certainly, there will be other dangers that lurk around corners in our lives. Since we are limited by our human five senses and natural knowledge, let us depend on God, his son Jesus Christ and the Holy Ghost to lead us, protect us, warn us and reveal what we cannot know on our own! God truly knows what is around every corner! He is an omniscient (all knowing, all seeing) God! There is none like our God! He is All Mighty, and nothing is too hard for our Awesome God!

* * *

When I finished writing this chapter, I shared this true story with my son Roger who is now grown. I was surprised when he stated that he remembered the situation. Although he was only five years old at the time, the sound of me screaming for him to stop and the image of that moving red pick-up truck that would have hit him, are etched into his memory. We both are truly grateful to God for sparing his life! The Lord is an on-time God who can reveal a danger and save you from it, in a split moment of time! Glory be to the name of the Lord!

Chapter 15

No Accident That Day!

Like most major cities, Atlanta, Georgia has its fair share of cars on any one of the major expressways. Atlanta has multiple major highways: I will only list five. There are two main expressways that facilitate travel north to south, I-75 and I-85; two that head east to west, I-20 and GA Highway 166 and the infamous circular I-285 that everyone gets lost on at least twice before they are considered acclimated to traveling around the city. I love that many of the expressways are tree-lined because trees have a way of making you feel calm.

One day I was driving on I-75 heading north driving about 55 miles per hour, which was the speed limit at the time. I planned to exit the highway at the next exit ramp, so I moved to the slowest lane. We were stopped because of a red traffic light at the top of the ramp. I was in a relaxed mood, listening to soft music and reflecting on the day's events as I waited for the long line of cars to start moving toward the exit ramp.

EYES OPENED Into The Supernatural World!

Suddenly, there was a loud crashing sound as my car was struck on the driver's side with such a strong force that my vehicle was horizontally knocked from the slowest lane where I was headed for the exit ramp, to the emergency lane! Please keep in mind that the emergency lane is parallel to the driving lanes. I did not understand how my car was hit on the driver's side on the expressway since all of the cars were traveling north. It was not like there was a cross street like on city streets where someone can T-bone you from the side, nor had there been an accident on my left.

I was shaken up because of the loud sound and the fact that my car was hit so hard. I assumed there would be significant damage on my side of the car because of how forcibly my vehicle was moved into the emergency lane.

Within three seconds of my vehicle being struck and forcibly moved to the emergency lane, five cars were hit from the rear to include the cars that previously had been waiting immediately in front of me and behind me. It was a multi-car smash up!

Cautiously, I opened my door and got out to assess what I felt would be a heavily damaged car on my driver's side. To my amazement, there was not one scratch or dent of any kind on the side of my car or any other area of my vehicle! I know this sounds crazy, but it is absolutely true. I could hardly believe it myself. I frowned and looked closer and there was no damage!

The other drivers were assessing their damage, shaking their heads, pulling out their cell phones, insurance, and registration cards. I looked at my perfectly spared car again and said to the female driver that had previously been in front of me, "Well, since I am not part of this accident, I am going to leave."

She said, "I don't blame you." The woman walked away with a disgusted expression, shaking her head.

I know sometimes things like accidents happen, but God intervened: and he did not allow me to be a part of that five-car collision! Let me tell you what I truly believe happened.

In an earlier chapter, I shared my experience of seeing two Heavenly Angels with my natural eyes, while I was in a church service. In this situation, I believe God sent an angel to miraculously, push my car horizontally out of the way three seconds before the multi-car pileup was going to happen. I know the crashing sound I heard and the force with which my car, with me in it, was completely moved into the next lane that was the emergency lane; was real and a miracle! There was no vehicle that crashed into me from the side to push me to that outer lane; therefore, it had to be an angel that forcibly moved me! Literally, seconds later, five cars were involved in the multi-car wreck that did not affect me because the car behind me did not hit me. It hit the vehicle that was previously in front of my car!

This is an example of the miracle-working power of God! He can certainly do whatever he wants to do when he wants to do it! I believe God and "his ability to do exceedingly and above what I can ask or think, according to the power that works in us." according to Ephesians 3:20. Do you believe in miracles? I believe in miracles and God's Divine Intervention! I can truly testify that the Lord has saved me from many calamities! Glory be to God!

Chapter 16

God Knows Who Needs Prayer

Have you ever been going through a difficult time in your life, but suddenly, you feel strength to press through the trouble? Perhaps you have felt that somebody was looking out for you and you were encouraged even though the circumstances that you were dealing with had not changed. Maybe there were people all over the country who were praying for you and the strength you felt was because of their prayers! Their prayers for you may have been unknown to you, but they were felt by you. These were prayers from people who were influenced by God through the Holy Spirit to intercede on your behalf!

Many times, the Lord Jesus has brought someone to my mind who I had not thought about in a while. God led me to intervene by sincerely praying for the person or one of his or her family members. Sometimes, I found out later why they needed prayer.

What I love about this is that in my worst times of suffering, I know for sure that the Lord had me in mind and he had people praying for me. I also know that the Lord Jesus intercedes or prays for us, while sitting on the right hand of God. Romans 8:34 says, "It is Christ who died, and furthermore is also risen, who is even at the right hand of God, who also makes intercession (prayer/prays) for us."

I know God has placed me on the hearts of others to pray for me. Through the years, some people have called to tell me and others I felt in my spirit were praying for me. Be encouraged my friends, you are not alone in this world no matter what you are dealing with in your life. God has you covered, and he has people who he uses to help you through the Spirit realm, to pray for you while you are on this journey of life!

Effective Prayers Work Across Miles

My Father's name was Clarence Milroe and he grew up as an only child, in Baton Rouge, Louisiana. He later migrated to Chicago, Illinois where he met and married my mother Gwendolyn Jolly Milroe. That is how I was born and raised in the Windy City.

My Father's God-Brother and best childhood friend is Claude Sanders who also migrated from Baton Rouge, Louisiana to Detroit, Michigan where he married his wife Bertha, and raised four sons.

Permetrice Milroe Jackson

Three are police officers or detectives (retired). During my entire life, my siblings and I called him, "Uncle Claude" which we fondly call him to this day. We have remained close to his family.

One night I went to sleep and started having a dream about a man who looked just like Uncle Claude. The near twin to him was very sick and in my dream, he was transported to a hospital in Detroit, Michigan. Since Uncle Claude had several brothers and they all look alike, I assumed that the dream was about one of them.

As I dreamed, I noticed that the man was admitted into the hospital and subsequently, he was moved to the intensive care unit. I knew he needed an intervention of intercessory prayer: therefore, I started praying for him in my dream. I continued to pray for him once I woke up because the dream was so realistic!

The next day, I was so concerned that I called Uncle Claude. Of course, I asked if he was okay as well as his brothers.

Uncle Claude stated, "It's good to hear from you. I am fine." I proceeded to share with him the dream that I had the night before. After I described the dream, he asked me, "Did somebody call you?"

I said, "No, sir. Nobody called me."

Uncle Claude then stated, "This is amazing! My brother was rushed by ambulance to the hospital last night and he is in intensive care. Since nobody called you, you must have a gift like Joseph in the Bible. You know, God showed Joseph things in dreams that he could not know on his own."

I replied, "Yes, you are right. God showed Joseph things in prophetic dreams." We continued our conversation as I marveled about how good God is to have his people intervene for others by praying about pertinent issues that we would not know if the Spirit did not reveal the information to us.

The Bible says in Acts 2:17, "In the last days, God says, I will pour out my Spirit on all people: and your sons and daughters will prophesy, and your young men will see visions, your old men will dream dreams." I am truly blessed to have experienced both; prophetic visions and God inspired dreams. I prayed for Uncle Claude's brother and once he was home from the hospital, I called to communicate with him. I believe that my prayers and those of others blessed him to survive. The Bible says in James 5:16, "...The effectual fervent (enthusiastic, passionate) prayers of the righteous avails (profits) much." In other word, our prayers are effective, anointed, and powerful! The precious prayers of God's people, positively impact lives!

I thank God that he is concerned enough about you, to lead someone from your family, church, neighborhood or even a family friend from the other side of the country to intervene in prayer for your miracle healing or other needs. God truly does care for you!

Chapter 17

God Still Speaks Today

According to the Bible in Genesis Chapter 1, God created the world in six days. In Genesis 2:2, we read that on the seventh day, God rested. God was modeling for us the principle of diligent work and the need for appropriate rest. To be clear, since God is a Spirit, he did not require rest, but he knew we would need to; therefore, he showed us or modeled for us, the way to have proper balance in life. Rest is extremely important, and you need to focus on ways to improve your sleep habits which can lead to a better you.

Getting enough sleep can help boost your immune system; strengthen your heart; improve your metabolism thereby helping you get and maintain a healthy body weight, reduces stress, helps you think clearly, regulates your mood, increases your exercise endurance and improves your overall mental and physical health. These are phenomenal benefits to you for simply giving your body the proper amount of rest and sleep.

Permetrice Milroe Jackson

You Need Rest for Your Mind

With so much going on in the world today, you also need to practice resting your mind and spirit. Jesus said in Matthew 11:28-30, "Come to me, all you who labor and are heavy laden, and I will give you rest. Take my yoke upon you, and learn from me, for I am gentle and lowly in heart, and you will find rest for your souls. For my yoke is easy and my burden is light." In other words, talk to the Lord about your problems and let him lead and guide you to help you solve them. Above and through it all, find ways to keep your peace of mind. We can achieve this because Isaiah 9:6 tells us that Jesus is the "…Prince of Peace," so don't let fear or anxiety control you!

Fear and anxiety can cripple your life and hinder your progress forward. Being gripped with fear and controlled by anxiety are why so many people are on prescription medications to calm their nerves. Break free today from the devil's attacks! We find in the Scripture, Philippians 4:6-7, "Do not be anxious (worried) about anything, but in every situation, by prayer, and supplication, with thanksgiving, let your requests be made known to God; and the peace of God, which surpasses all understanding, will guard your hearts and minds through Christ Jesus."

When you are stressed out, find a way to focus on yourself, your family and whatever is important to you. Take one day at a time. No matter what you are dealing with, God assures us that he will not allow more to come on you than what you can handle. We read in 1 Corinthians 10:13, "No temptation (test or trial) has overtaken you except such as is common to man; but God is faithful, who will not allow you to be tempted (or tested) beyond what you are able to stand, but with the temptation will also make a way of escape, that you may be able to bear it."

Please know that if you need extra help, it is okay to reach out to a pastor, minister, counselor, or a therapist to assist you in dealing with the stresses of life! You do not have to suffer in silence. It is all part of selfcare, and you deserve to have peace and tranquility. As you take care of yourself, you will ensure that you are physically healthy, as well as mentally, emotionally, and spiritually balanced. As you get your entire life together, you are better equipped to take care of your family and others.

Jesus said in Matthew 22:35-39, "Love the Lord your God with all your heart and with all your soul and with all your mind. That is the first and greatest commandment. And the second is like it: Love your neighbor as yourself." As you love and properly care for yourself, you can better love and care for others.

Permetrice Milroe Jackson

How Do You Get to Know a Living God?

It is important to have a meaningful and fulfilling life. Since we are spirit, soul, and body, we need to make developing our relationship with God in a real and intimate way, a priority above anyone or anything else.

How do you get to know a living God? Once you give your life to the Lord Jesus Christ, you start developing your relationship with him through personal prayer, reading and studying his Word the Bible, attending a good Bible-believing church for teaching, instruction and fellowship as well as sincerely living for God.

When you live for God, it is vitally important to fellowship with him through a dedicated and consistent prayer life! When you pray to God, you are talking to, or communicating with him. It is a two-way exchange. God can respond to you in many ways. The Bible says in John 4:24, "God is Spirit and those who worship him, must worship in spirit and in truth." Your carnal flesh does not comprehend the things of the Spirit, but your willing spirit wants to and can choose to agree with the Spirit of God. That agreement helps you grow spiritually as you progress in the Christian Faith; it strengthens your personal relationship with Jesus and enhances your walk with the Lord everyday of your life!

God Speaks to Your Spirit

God has spoken to me in various ways. Sometimes he speaks to my spirit in what some phrase as, "the still, small voice" of God. In other words, it's inward, but clear enough to be heard by your "inner ear" with precision. All I can say is that for you to experience this, your spirit must be one with God through his Son Jesus Christ, praying to or communicating with him, so that you can hear what the Spirit of God whispers into your connected and receptive spirit.

Though Rare, God Speaks Audibly

God can speak any time and in any way that he chooses to speak to you. Although it is rare that God speaks to individuals audibly or out loud, he may speak in an audible voice to you. It is up to God. I know because I have had the unique experience of hearing God speak to me in an audible voice!

There are times in the Bible where God spoke to individuals in an audible voice. One example is when God spoke and called a young man's name and he thought it was a physical man calling him. Three times the young man checked with the Prophet in the house: however, it was not a human being calling him. We read in 1 Samuel 3:8-10, "And the Lord called Samuel a third time. And Samuel got up and went to Eli and said, "Here am I, you called me." Then Eli realized that the Lord was calling the boy. Eli told Samuel, "Go and lie down, and if he calls you say, 'Speak Lord, for your servant is listening.' So, Samuel went and lay down in his place. And the Lord came, and stood, and called as at other times, "Samuel, Samuel." Then Samuel answered, "Speak; for thy servant hears." God called Samuel in an audible voice, but he thought it was Eli. This is an awesome example of God speaking to someone in an audible voice!

God Knows How to Get Your Attention

God may use extraordinary methods to get your attention. When he wanted to talk to Moses to give him instructions reference to delivering his people from bondage, God caused a bush to burn with fire, without the fire consuming the bush! In Exodus 3:1-20, the Bible tells us that this remarkable sight stopped Moses, who walked over to the bush to get a better view. Once God had his attention, God spoke in an audible voice in Exodus 3:5 saying,

"Moses take off your shoes from off your feet; for the ground you stand on is Holy ground."

Some of you may think that was just for those early, back in the Bible days, but Hebrews 13:8 says, "Jesus Christ is the same yesterday, today and forever." Since Jesus Christ or the Anointed One, is the Son of God and they are One, we know God does not change. In Malachi 3:6 the Word says, "For I am the Lord, I change not; therefore, you sons of Jacob are not destroyed." Since God spoke audibly to people then, he can and does speak audibly or out loud to people now! Remember, it is up to God.

God's Voice is Majestic

I feel so honored to be one of God's vessels that he uses in the earth. I humbly submit my life to him to be a Woman of God. He speaks to me, but he also speaks through me. When I am invited to be a guest speaker in a church, I pray and seek God in-order-to be led by him to know what to teach. God knows who will be in the audience and what their needs are. When I stand to deliver an anointed message in a church, I have already prepared the sermon and I let the Lord use me.

Many times, after preaching the Word of God, he uses me to speak a Prophetic Word of Knowledge to individuals, which usually confirms something that they have been asking God about in prayer. Sometimes, God uses me to give people direction, or he reveals insight into personal or business affairs to advise or warn them about important issues or concerns. The Lord also reveals sensitive information to me about people that I share with them in their ear rather than over the microphone because it is their personal business. All these examples of me hearing from God are because I listen to what God is saying and by faith, I say what he tells me to say.

When I first heard God speak to me in an audible voice, it was so clear that I almost thought somebody was in the house with me. I realized that nobody was at home with me; therefore, I knew it was God speaking. Hearing God's voice was an amazing and life-changing experience!

When I first heard God speak to my spirit, it was just as clear as his audible voice, but it was inward, not out loud. This was many years ago; and I must admit that I had to learn his voice. The Bible says in John 10:27, "My sheep know my voice and I know them, and they follow me." And, verse John 10:5 says, "and a stranger they will not follow, but will flee from him: for they know not the voice of him." We must be careful to whom we listen to and follow.

EYES OPENED Into The Supernatural World!

There may be many people giving you advice and each one may have sincere intentions, but make sure that you seek God and listen to his voice and guidance. One scripture that I love is Proverbs 3:5-6 which says, "Trust in the Lord with all your heart; and lean not on your own understanding. In all your ways acknowledge him and he will direct your paths." Notice that this word path is plural. That means every area of your life is important enough for God to care about guiding you so that you will get to the right destiny, fulfill his intentional purpose for your life and that you will be richly blessed!

God knows what is best for you and he also has the ability to see around every curve, fork-in-the-road, or blocked path; therefore, as you seek him earnestly, his guidance is critical to your overall peace, prosperity, natural or business success in this life. Trust God because he really does care for you!

Listen for His Instructions

Listen to God when he speaks to you. It could be through his "still small voice" or it could be through the Scriptures when you are reading the Bible. God may send you a message through the mouth of an innocent child who lovingly says just what you need to hear. God may give you a profound and explicit dream that you vividly remember when you wake up.

God may inspire a minister to preach a sermon so tailored to your situation that you feel as if they know what is going on in your life, household, business, or place of employment. God may allow a visiting guest speaker to say a Word of Knowledge or Prophetic Word to you that you realize they could not humanly know without God's revelation.

God may even choose to allow you to be an honored recipient of his very Presence and hear his awesome audible voice. If you are ever privileged and blessed to hear his audible voice, I guarantee you this rare experience will make an indelible impact on your life!

God Truly Loves You

Whichever way God chooses to talk to or communicate with you, know that he loves you and he wants to have fellowship with you. He cares enough to be attentive to your praise. The Bible says in Psalms 22:3, "God inhabits the praise of his people." In other words, your praise gets God's attention. As you live for God, we also know that God listens to your prayer requests because the Bible says in 1 Peter 3:12, "For the eyes of the Lord are over the righteous, and his ears are attentive (open) to their prayers: but the face of the Lord is against them who do (or practice) evil."

Be encouraged and know that God loves you and he cares about the details of your life. As you walk with God, understand that even when you are in a struggle, you are not alone. The Bible says in Psalm 34:17-18, "The righteous cry, and the Lord hears, and delivers them out of all their troubles. The Lord is near unto them that are of a broken heart; and saves such as be of a contrite (remorseful or repented) spirit." Glory be to God!

As you seek God and become stronger in the Christian faith, God may give you - Eyes Opened Into the Supernatural World! Make your relationship with God an intentional priority and watch him bless your life in a phenomenal way, in Jesus' Name!

God's Plan of Salvation:

God loves you and he wants a relationship with you. He sent his son Jesus to die for your sins. The Bible says in **John 3:16, "For God so loved the world, that he gave his only begotten Son, that whosoever believeth in him should not perish, but have everlasting life."** The phrase "believeth in him" (Jesus) means to trust in and lean on him. God made a way for you to live for and walk with him as you live your life.

Prayer to give your life to God through Jesus:

God, I have sinned in my life and I am sorry for the wrong I have done. I ask that you forgive me and change me. Help me live a life that pleases you. I believe that Jesus Christ is the Son of God and I accept him as my Lord and Savior. Wash me with the precious blood of Jesus Christ, which was shed for my sins. Deliver me from all unrighteousness and sin, and help me live for you, in Jesus' name. Amen.

EYES OPENED Into The Supernatural World!

After Your Prayer:

If you sincerely prayed the above prayer, you are saved. The Bible says, **in Romans 10:9, "If you will confess with your mouth Jesus is Lord and believe in your heart that God raised him from the dead, you will be saved."** Join and faithfully attend a good Bible believing, teaching church. Start reading your Bible every day or as often as you can. The New Testament would be a great place to start. Remember to pray, which is simply communication with God the Father, Jesus Christ the Son of God, and the Holy Ghost or Holy Spirit. Praise God every day because he is worthy of your praise! The Bible says in **Psalm 150:6, "Let everything that has breath, praise the Lord! Praise the Lord!"** Sincerely serve the Lord Jesus Christ and grow spiritually through the Grace of God! Be Blessed!

Permetrice Milroe Jackson

About the Author

Permetrice Milroe Jackson is an author of intriguing novels. The latest is entitled *Duplicity: Double Life Drama,* which is available in paperback and eBook formats. She is currently finishing a Thriller Novel. She also wrote the inspirational and anointed book, *Rejoice After Rejection!* This book encourages people to process the pain of relationship rejection, heal and learn how to press forward to a blessed future rejoicing! She also has a booklet entitled *Effective Prayers in Jesus' Name.* She is a minister of the Gospel and a seasoned conference and revival speaker. Permetrice is a poet who is often asked to write original poems for various Christian services and other social events. She is an actress and has performed in Gospel stage plays in Atlanta, Georgia. Permetrice has also been interviewed on various cable programs such as Atlanta's TV57 WATC, *Atlanta Live Program* and local broadcast news channel FOX 5 Atlanta.

Permetrice earned a Bachelor of Arts Degree in Business Administration with a Concentration in Marketing from Clark Atlanta University in Atlanta, Georgia. She had an illustrious career with the Federal

Government, Department of the Army, where she personally worked with active duty, one, two and three-star army generals, teaching them various computer skills as well as the use of other technology equipment. Permetrice served as a Division Chief and supervised military officers and enlisted soldiers. Although they are usually supervised and rated by senior military members, the Lieutenant Colonel trusted her leadership and appointed her as the Division Chief.

As the Division Chief, Permetrice traveled extensively across the Southeast United States to support 72 subordinate offices, ensuring procedural compliance with official federal regulations. She also led automation and communications inspections at various military installations. Permetrice resigned to pursue her dream of devoting more time with her children. She later answered the call to evangelistic ministry.

Currently, Permetrice is a highly qualified, certified high school teacher. She loves motivating her students to work hard and to make great decisions so that they develop into life-long learners who are academically and personally ready for college, professional careers, entrepreneurship, and successful lives.

As a minister of the Gospel, Evangelist Permetrice Milroe Jackson preaches and teaches with a profound depth of knowledge, interpreting the

Permetrice Milroe Jackson

Greek and Hebrew languages as they relate to Bible Scriptures. She expounds on the Word of God with simplicity so that the youngest in attendance can clearly understand the lesson. When led by God, she speaks Prophetic Words of Knowledge to the people of God confirming his will. The Lord has anointed Permetrice to walk in the position of a Prophetess and "Seer" with the gift of seeing into the supernatural realm. Permetrice served in one local ministry for 19½ years, was a staff and platform minister as well as an Elder of the church. While there, she worked with the ministry telecast director, recording voice-overs for the broadcast production for over four years. With her pastor's blessing, she stepped out by faith to pastor a church for a season of over five years. As the Lord opens doors, Evangelist Jackson speaks in various churches, delivering powerful and anointed messages to bless the people of God in revivals, women's conferences, and youth programs.

To contact the author for speaking engagements, please send correspondence to the address of the publisher or you may contact her at pmjatlanta@yahoo.com. Permetrice would love for you to follow her on Twitter and Instagram @pmjatlanta.

EYES OPENED Into The Supernatural World!

Notes:_____

_____

_____

_____

_____

_____

_____

_____

_____

_____

_____

_____

_____

_____

_____

_____

_____

_____